CHEESE
ROLLING
IN GLOUCESTERSHIRE

CHEESE ROLLING
IN GLOUCESTERSHIRE

JEAN JEFFERIES

TEMPUS

Frontispiece: An unknown spectator. (Jean Jefferies)

First published 2007

Tempus Publishing Limited
The Mill, Brimscombe Port,
Stroud, Gloucestershire, GL5 2QG
www.tempus-publishing.com

British Library Cataloguing in Publication Data.
A catalogue record for this book is available from the British Library.

ISBN 97807524 4302 7

Typesetting and origination by Tempus Publishing Limited.
Printed in Great Britain.

Contents

Foreword

One of the many reasons why I've fallen hopelessly in love with Gloucestershire is the fact we live in a county teeming with ancient festivals that nowhere else can match. Just say the word, and we're off elver eating, well dressing, shin kicking, and woolsack racing but top of the list has always been cheese rolling on Cooper's Hill. It's the only activity that attracts television crews from all over the world and every year, without fail, leaves you breathless with a mixture of disbelief, anxiety and pride. This book takes you on a journey through time – you'll discover nuggets of information that'll add to the mystery, surprise you and ultimately reaffirm why there's no other event on earth like it. Having read the following few pages and you next look up Cooper's Hill, you might well see Iron-Age tribes and Romans at the top, a Brockworth virgin spinning down, and when the cheese lands at your feet you'll know exactly how it's made. Read how the event overcame rationing, foot-and-mouth disease and baffling bureaucracy to become what it is today. Enjoy this definitive guide celebrating eccentricity, bravery, stupidity and sheer, unadulterated fun.

Mark Cummings,
BBC Radio Gloucestershire

Introduction

This all began when I decided to update the leaflet that is handed to spectators as they arrive in the car park. The question that everyone asks is 'When did it all start?' I confidently set out to find the answer. Nine years later I have come to the conclusion that nobody will ever know. I traced it back to the 1800s when it was, even then, an ancient tradition.

Cooper's Hill today is a small community. When transport was by way of foot or pack horse, the Cheese Rolling and Wake would have been a celebration for local agricultural workers and craftsmen. People might have come from as far away as Brockworth, Bentham, Birdlip, Hucclecote, Shurdington and Cranham (all within a radius of about 5 miles). I wonder who else would have known that it was happening and who they would have told? Who would have written it all down?

It seems that we can show when it was definitely happening but the lack of written records do not prove that it wasn't taking place many many years before.

Jean Jefferies,
2007

Acknowledgements

This book wrote itself with a great deal of help from many people. My thanks go to:

The Cheese Rolling Committee; Liz and Richard Ashenden; Gordon Baylis; Olive Bushell; Anne Cooke; Rosemary Cooke; Nigel Cox, curator Gloucester Folk Museum; Mark Cummings (www.bbc.co.uk/gloucestershire); Spencer Feeney, past editor of *The Citizen*; Peggy Forrester; Brian Firth; Gisèle Guarisco-Jefferies; staff at the Gloucestershire Collection (local studies); Rosemary (Jean) Hellerman; Christopher Holiday; John Hudson (www.avsglos.com); *The Japan Times*; Martin Kirby, *The Citizen*; Ginette and Richard Landesberg; John Lovell, *The Citizen*; Joy Macdonald; Gloria and Walla Mander; Lilla McGrory; Ian Mean, editor, *The Citizen*; Margaret and Dave Miller; Roy Mitchell and family; Bill Organ; Clare Parrack (www.thisisgloucester-shire); Iris Peasley and the late Tony Peasley; Maureen and Tony Pither; Mike Price; Paul Quarry; Eleanor Rawlings (née Hicks); Anita Syvret, editor, *The Gloucestershire Echo*; Janet Whitton; WI House; Harold Wingham; the late John Yates (BBC), Jeremy Kaye and Malcolm Hopkins.

I hope I have included all the people without whose help this could never have been compiled. I apologise for any omissions.

A great deal of the information that has been used has come from personal scrapbooks and photograph albums which are the property of local Cooper's Hill and Brockworth residents, as well as others.

It has not been possible to identify with certainty the original source of many of the articles and photographs that appear in this Cheese Rolling history. Articles that appeared in publications in the past have been trimmed and consequently give no details of their origins, while photographs have been carefully stuck in albums, giving no indication of their photographers. I have done my best to give credit to authorship wherever possible.

one

Where is Cooper's Hill?

Cooper's Hill stands on the western edge of the Gloucestershire Cotswolds about 6 miles from Cheltenham and 5 miles from Gloucester. It is south-east of Brockworth, the nearest village (approximately 1 mile away), on the A46 Cheltenham to Painswick and Stroud road. The lane that follows the contours of the hill through the hamlet forms part of the Cotswold Way which runs from Bath to Chipping Camden and is a popular route for walkers. Another lane crossing the Cotswold Way and running up the hill is Green Street. This was once part of the ancient Salt Way used for transporting salt on pack animals from Bristol to the Midlands.

The hill itself has seen many peoples come and go. There is some speculation that Phoenicians came to the area. If so, they would have been here in about 1200-1100 BC. The Iron Age encampment that was in existence about 500 BC was possibly inhabited by the Dobunni tribe. It was one of the largest camps in Gloucestershire being at least 200 acres in area, situated between Cooper's Hill and Cranham. It was scheduled as an Ancient Monument in 1979. The Romans lived in the area from about AD 45-410. The site and remains of a Roman villa stand at Witcombe less than a mile away from Cooper's Hill and the progeny of the giant edible Roman snail still roam the area. Remains of a mediaeval village have been discovered between Cooper's Hill and Birdlip, about 2 miles away.

On the occasions when beacons have been lit around the country, at least six have been seen from the hill at Malvern, Bredon, Cleeve Hill, Painswick, Forest of Dean and May Hill. The north-facing slope has a 1:2 incline (in places even 1:1) which is 200yds long, clear of trees and a prominent landmark, visible from many miles around.

This slope is the site of the annual Cheese Rolling and Wake and at the summit of the hill a maypole marks the venue. At the highest point is Cooper's Hill Common. All the land owned by Gloucestershire County Council and forming part of the reserve has been registered as common land. Its use as common land goes back well before the tenth century and is suggested to have been land which was used by everyone 'in common' for grazing, hunting, collecting firewood and so on. These uses have become, by common use, 'rights'.

An engraving from Sir Robert Atkyn's *Gloucestershire*, 1712, with Witcombe Park on the lower slopes of Cooper's Hill on the left.

At the foot of the slope is the hamlet of Cooper's Hill. In the 1841 census there were twenty-six dwellings listed – this included the lower slopes of Cooper's Hill as well as the hamlet itself. Owners of these properties on the hill holding these rights were the commoners. These commoners' rights, which vary for different dwellings, include:

Herbage or pasture (the right to graze horses, cattle, sheep, goats or geese)
Estovers (the right to gather wood for fuel)
Turbary (the right to dig turf for roofing or fuel)
Pannage (the right to let pigs loose to forage for acorns or beech mast)

In 1970, Cooper's Hill became the first local nature reserve in south-west England. The following report made at a meeting of the Upton St Leonards Parish Council, appeared in *The Citizen* of 7 January 1970:

The 137-acre area designated is included in the Upton and Brockworth parishes ... there were a number of unique features on the land, which mainly comprised Brockworth and Upton Woods, a limestone quarry and thorn scrub ... it is an example of the original beech on the Cotswold escarpment, and there is the natural encroachment of the beech on to open land ... a large selection of more or less all British mammals, except the deer (at least two species of deer are now to be seen in the area of the hill and common), and over 200 species of plants. Existing footpaths would be cleared where necessary through the scrub to provide a guided walk in the Brockworth section ... it would not be developed for any recreational purposes which are incompatible with a reserve ... the area will be the County Council's entry in the 1970 European Conservation Year and will probably become a national reserve ... the limestone from the quarry was used mainly for agricultural purposes until 1965, when the amount of limestone had dropped ... the council bought the whole quarry's ownership in 1967.

Three views taken from the top of Cooper's Hill:

Looking towards Cheltenham, 1939.

Brockworth, 1935 (Hucclecote is further left). It is also possible to see the gorse attached halfway up the pole left over from that year's Wake on 29 May. Just below the hill is the Gloucester Aircraft Co. It later became the premises of ICI and in 2006, Invista.

Brockworth with the Invista factory on the left, 2005. (Jean Jefferies)

The Citizen of 11 June quoted:

> Cooper's Hill, famous for its Cheese Rolling, beautiful landscape and breathtaking views, became the first local nature reserve in the south-west today. It will eventually become part of a larger national nature reserve.
>
> It is a joint venture in European Conservation Year between the Gloucestershire Trust for Nature Conservation, the Nature Conservancy Council, South West Region, and the Planning Department of the County Council. It is not meant to be a recreation area – its prime purpose is to inform the public of the natural history of the area.
>
> [The reserve lies within the Cotswolds Area of Outstanding Natural Beauty (AONB).]

On 27 May 1974 at the annual Cheese Rolling and Wake, concerns of the organising committee were voiced about the erosion of the centre of the hill caused by people walking up and down throughout the year. The committee feared that the hill was becoming dangerous to the competitors and that the event could be stopped in future. As the hill was common land, people were entitled to walk it. It would be difficult to fill the path that had appeared as the rain would wash fresh turf away. The crevice was being used by the public to get to the nature trail at the top. The organising committee suggested the possibility of having to fence off the slope.

In May 1978 fears were once more expressed that the annual Cheese Rolling could end because of the damage and erosion of the face of the hill, and the possible danger to those taking part. It was decided to cancel the uphill race.

The county land agent, Mr Geoffrey Wyatt, issued a statement that explained the reasons for the continuing damage. He said that the bare face of Cooper's Hill was slipping because it was part of the Cotswold scarp which was unstable. It was slipping faster than other parts because it was not covered by vegetation. Heavy use was preventing the natural growth recovering. The county council had been aware of the problem for a number of years and three years earlier they had tried to improve the drainage at the top of the face and improve the grass. The attempts met with failure however, because they could not keep people off the grass for long enough. The county council refuted the suggestion that the nature trail had any effect on the Cheese Rolling slope.

Above: Aerial view. (R. Cooke)

Right: The present sign of The Cheeserollers pub. (Jean Jefferies)

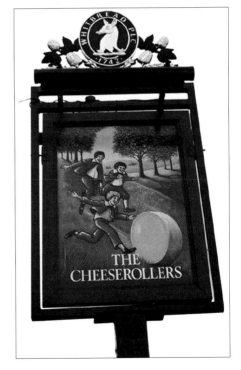

On 16 August 1978, restoration proposals were made for the famous Cheese Rolling slope. Gloucestershire County Council planned to erect fences at the top and bottom of the slope, fill in the ruts and divots and reseed the grass. It was said that the fences would be removed for the Cheese Rolling ceremonies and taken away permanently after three years (they were eventually removed in August 2004). The slope was being eroded by people walking on it. One councillor said that it was the only piece of history left in the area and the committee chairman added that the annual Cheese Rolling was a famous custom that must be preserved.

In 1979 the Iron Age encampment was scheduled as an Ancient Monument.

In 2001 the area was recommended as a Special Area of Conservation (SAC) because, 'it contains habitat types and/or species which are rare or threatened a European context'.

In Shurdington, a village (on the A46) between Brockworth and Cheltenham, is an inn that was originally called the New Inn. In July 1975 the owners, Whitbread Flowers, decided that the New Inn had ceased to be new. They renamed it the Cheeserollers to mark the annual event. Col. W.J. Davis, at that time chairman of the Cooper's Hill Cheese Rolling Committee, unveiled the sign.

two

Origins and Development

There seem to be no early records of Cooper's Hill Cheese Rolling and Wake. Local folklore claims that the rolling of a cheese may have prehistoric origins and symbolism. That part of the hill where the rolling takes place is in shadow for much of the year – perhaps there was a ceremony to celebrate the summer solstice. It is generally understood that the ceremony was originally held at midsummer.

Who First Sent Missiles Rolling Down Cooper's Hill?

One theory is that it may have been introduced by the Phoenicians when they sailed up the Bristol Channel on trading expeditions. The *Children's Britannica* says, 'Phoenicia was an ancient country covering what are now Syria and Lebanon in the Middle East. The Phoenicians were the only Semitic tribe to become seafaring people ... they were great traders and people of all nations bought from them'.

A reference in 1931 to Professor Robertson-Smith's book on *The History of Israel* tells how, 'every village in Canaan had on a high place, an altar to Baal, the god of agriculture and by the side of it was erected what in Bible language is called a grove.' He says that grove is a wrong translation for the roughly carved head of Baal which formed the top of the pole just over the altar of Baal. Baal was a powerful warrior god in the Biblical land of Canaan and a rival for the Israelite god Yahweh (Jehovah). The Phoenicians sailed from Syria's coast from about 1200 BC.

Professor Robertson-Smith said that when the Phoenicians came to the south-west of England they brought some of their gods with them and set up their altars and poles surmounted by the head of the god, on the 'high places'.

At the highest point of Cooper's Hill – looking across the valley to the River Severn – stands a maypole topped by a golden cockerel. Was this originally a pole topped by the head of Baal? The reference goes on to quote Sir James G. Frazer, FRS, FBA in his book *The Golden Bough, A Study in Magic and Religion*. He notes that in all the Phoenician religions the priest at the Spring

Festival used to make discs of 'withies', take them up, set them on fire, and roll them down the hill from the 'high place' dedicated to Baal'.

Sir James Frazer describes numerous ancient festivals and customs, any one of which could have been the origin we are seeking.

Perhaps this is the true origin, the discs now having been replaced by a cheese. This seems to be a most attractive and exciting explanation! It has been said, however, that if the Phoenicians were trading along the Cornish coast, there really was no reason for them to navigate around the peninsular and sail up the Bristol Channel.

However, doubt has recently been cast on whether the Phoenicians even reached mainland Britain at all. It seems that they might only have landed on the Isles of Scilly. The Ancient Britons (possibly the Dobunni) of the Iron Age, held midsummer ceremonials that often took the form of fire rituals. Lighted wheels were rolled down hillsides and lighted discs were hurled through the air. A statement made by Michael James in his article entitled *The Origins of Cheese Rolling on Cooper's Hill'* (date unknown) says that:

A perusal of county records reveals the Cheese Rolling ceremony was taking place over 1,300 years ago. In those times the ceremony took place at Midsummer, until the Anglo-Saxon authorities altered the time to Whitsuntide. Although not actually documented, this suggests an attempt by the clergy to allay, or eliminate, a religion far older than Christianity. Some authorities will argue Christianity was already well established in Britain by this time, but a study of any encyclopaedia will establish this was not so. Ancient beliefs, including various forms of witchcraft, were still being practised in the late nineteenth century and, in fact, in some places, are still flourishing today.

Confirmation of the pagan origins of Cheese Rolling can be evaluated when comparison is made to similar ceremonies in Britain. Cheeses used to be rolled from the feet of the Uffington White Horse into the field below and at the Cerne Giant – another prehistoric chalk carving – a like custom was performed.

At Wyeley in Staffordshire, a fiery wheel is rolled down the hillside at dead of night.

It is interesting to note that the fields at the bottom of all these slopes contain springs. At the bottom of Cooper's Hill there is a freshwater spring.

Authorities of pagan religions state a spring represents the renewal of life and the disc is the universal symbol of the sun; therefore the ceremonies are symbolic of the death and rebirth of the year.

After Midsummer the early people believed the sun was 'dying' but would be rejuvenated by the 'Spring of Life' in the underworld so it could return again in the spring.

A disc or wheel can also represent the undying circle of seasons.

In this context the scattering of sweets at the Cooper's Hill Cheese Rolling could well symbolise the fertility rite that would ensure a bountiful harvest.

A suggestion has been made in the past that perhaps Brockworth virgins were launched down the hill in wickerwork cages, a Cotswold variation of the colourful Druid ceremony described by Julius Caesar. Were cartwheels decorated with gorse set alight and rolled down? Gorse was until recent years tied to the centre of the maypole to ward off evil spirits and ensure a good harvest.

Kenneth Hare, writing in his book *Gloucestershire* around the 1940s suggests:

The sport dates back to the early Middle Ages, when it was inaugurated to protect the common-land about the maypole with its valuable grazing rights from inclosure. My theory is that this sport was in effect, in the first instance, a species of acted round-robin. The object of that form of petition is to make it impossible to guess who first applied his signature. So with the rolling. It must have been a keen-sighted man who detected the first trespasser amongst a hundred roaring rustics hunting a cheese!

A leaflet, produced by the Gloucestershire County Planning Department, titled *Cooper's Hill Local Nature Reserve* says about the Cheese Rolling:

From time immemorial each Whit Monday cheeses have been rolled down the hill from near the maypole. This custom is undoubtedly very old and is thought by some to have its origins in the ceremonies connected with worshipping the sun; the cheese representing the sun. Certainly the Cheese Rolling ceremonies held here used to be on mid-summer's day. Ceremonies, some similar to this one, were practised in many hillside villages in Gloucestershire and Wiltshire to mark the beginning of the cheese-making season.

A story is told of a Gloucestershire landlord who, generations ago, attempted to take away the common rights of Cooper's Hill. So strenuous were the protests of the villagers that he relented but he made it a condition that they roll a cheese down the hill every year.

It seems possible, therefore, that the ceremony perpetuated the ancient grazing rights of the commoners.

Glevensis, a 1977 publication of the Gloucester & District Archaeological Research Group, has another (maybe tongue-in-cheek) theory:

By the early eighteenth century, and no doubt, for centuries before, the hill was a major source of stone for the surrounding area. At the top of the High Brotheridge at the Cooper's Hill end, quarrying has been fairly extensive, so it is possible that use was made of the hill's one-in-one slope by clearing part of it and making it into a natural incline, to lower stone down to where the scarp levels out and transporting becomes easier.

Building hypothesis onto hypothesis, in the time-honoured way of Folk Lore Historians, I now put forward an alternative origin for the Cheese Rolling Festivities. Boys being boys, and youthful medieval labourers or apprentice quarrymen being no exception, they sought every opportunity to demonstrate their bravado to their elders, peers and – more likely – to comely local maidens.

Is it then simply that the agency of time has changed an individual's flamboyant pursuit of a casually released round stone, to a community's Cheese Rolling Wake, and finally to the Committee organised bank holiday Jamboree it is today?

According to Roy Palmer in *Folklore of Gloucestershire*, a document of 1680 on the subject of wakes mentions Cranham and Coaley but not Cooper's Hill, and the classic local histories of the eighteenth and nineteenth centuries ignore it. It certainly existed by the early 1800s. The apparent lack of early written records does not prove, however, that the event was not happening.

A paper sent to the Gloucester town crier in 1836 with a request to proclaim 'the annual sports of Whitsuntide' sheds light not only on the event but on local pronunciation:

Cooper's Hill Weke to commence on Wits Monday per sisly at 3 o'clock
2 cheese to be ron for.
1 Plain Cake to be green for. ('grinning' or 'gurning')
1 do. do. to be jumpt in the bag for. (sack race?)
Horings (oranges) to be Dipt in the toob for. (like apple'bobbing?)
Set of ribbons to be dansed for.
Belt to be rosled (wrestled) for.
A bladder of snuff to be chatred (chattered) for by hold wimming. (old women)

An article (probably in *The Citizen* or *The Gloucester Journal*) entitled *100 Years Ago* quotes from
The Gloucester Journal of 14 June 1884:

The annual wake was held at Cooper's Hill on Monday. The most interesting feature of the
amusements was the bowling of the cheese down the somewhat steep slope of the hill.

In 1890 H.Y.J. Taylor (born in 1828) wrote:

Some of my earliest recollections are associated with Cooper's Hill Wake, which, in old days, was
a festivity of some magnitude. Old John Jones, of Cooper's Hill, and the late Sir William Hicks, of
Witcomb Park, were great patrons of the annual saturnalia. I can recollect Organ, the master of
Ceremonies, who was a fine, tall, handsome fellow. He used to appear upon the summit of the hill,
dressed in a white linen chemise (smock), adorned with ribbons of all the colours of the rainbow.
His hat was also decked with ribbons, and around his waist he wore the belt for which the wrestlers
were to struggle, the winner claiming honour as the champion wrestler for the year. Organ's advent
was hailed with shouts by the hilarious multitude: and no Caesar attired in Imperial robe of Tyrian
dye could have been more proud than he was of his milk-white 'smock', for the old English name
and the Frenchified 'chemise' was that by which the garment was known to all:

> At the wake of Cooper's Hill
> Each Jack appeared with charming Jill.

In days of yore, not only the daughters of the peasants, but those also of the farmers, mingled
in the throng of merry dancers, and how proud were 'Jane' and 'Mary' of the ribbons they had
won by their agility and endurance!
   I have seen a couple of stalwart fellows, with sinew and tendon of iron, struggle fiercely, not
to say ferociously for the mastery. What a shout of exultation went up when the victor landed
his opponent fairly on his back on the sward! It was surprising how human limbs could be
strained and kicked without the thews cracking and the bones breaking. These brutal trials of
strength may have made the race hardy, tough, and valiant. To me, however, the spectacle was
brutal and inhuman.
   I once met an aged athlete, who had been the champion on Cooper's Hill, but had become
a cripple:
   'John', I asked, 'what is the matter?'
   'Why, Mayster Harry, I ha' got a nashun bod leg.'
   'How is that John?'
   'Mayster Harry, the follies o' my youth. If I had my days to go over agen, I'd never stond up
to ha' my legs kicked to pieces at Cooper's Hill wake. I ha' larned this, thot our blessed meeker

nivver made our precious limbs to be kicked at vor other volks' amusement.' The grinning through 'hosses' collards' was a grand amisement. Some of the faces distorted to produce the 'best grin' would have puzzled Lavater and delighted Hogarth.

Dipping in a tub of water for oranges and apples, and bobbing for penny loaves smeared with treacle, need no description.

The grand climax to the annual revel was running down the frightful declivity of a hill after a cheese. It was a perilous feat, but young fellows were ever willing to risk the danger.

An old man described the cheese as being 'hard as fayrur's (Pharaoh's) heart or the nether millstone.' I have seen the cheese bound down the hill and over a stone wall into the ground beyond. I have seen it in the hands of the winner without the symptom of a crack in it or the sign of an abrasion. To have run down the descent was perilous; to have eaten the trophy must have been a more dangerous feat than its capture.

Racing for the prize chemise was to me the most degrading part of the revel; but there were plenty of girls eager for the contest until a sad catastrophe occurred. On one occasion a young woman outpaced her competitors and reached the goal first – and there dropped dead.

Happily, the schoolmaster had been abroad among our rural as well as our town populations; the village flower-show has superseded the bouts at wrestling and grinning; and Cooper's Hill wake is numbered among the things that have been, and is now only a memory to those who have crossed the summit of life's journey.

So the events which had formed an important part of the 'Wake', or 'Festival' until then, (such as wrestling, grinning, sack-racing, chattering, and dancing for ribbons) had come to an end, to be replaced by a flower show.

Other events began: a tug of war between men and women (20 men and 40 women, with the women always winning!), climbing the maypole and coconut shies. The cheese, however, continued to roll on! H.Y.J. Taylor was a local historian. He died in January 1906 at the age of seventy-nine years.

A report in *The Gloucester Journal* of 25 January 1908 gives details of a special parish council meeting held to discuss the future of Cooper's Hill. The Common had been sold no less than three times during the previous three or four years and there had, 'always been considerable difference of opinion on the part of those who had purchased the Common and the Commoners, as to what the rights of the Commoners were.' It seems that the new purchaser, Mr Hanson-Powell, had 'suggested certain enclosures'. The parishioners, however, 'wanted particularly to guard very jealously the holding of Cooper's Hill Wake on the spot where it had been held for many years'. Mr William Brookes who at that time had for many years officiated as Master of Ceremonies at the Cooper's Hill Wake said:

This Wake has been where Mr Powell wants to take in [laughter and applause]. He is not going to do it. I have heard my father talk about the wake, and his father told him that his grandfather remembered it. That is 300 years ago, and I can go further back than that.

This would seem to be a reference to William's great-great-grandfather. Mr Brookes was at this time aged forty-seven, having been born in 1851. The Cooper's Hill census of 1841 records that George Brookes, aged forty, his wife Sarah, aged forty and their son John, aged twenty, were residents. William Brookes was John's son, so George who was born in 1801 was the grandfather he mentioned and his great-grandfather and great-great-grandfather are unnamed.

Unknown – approx 1750 (great-great-grandfather)
Unknown – approx 1775 (great-grandfather)

George Brookes – 1801 (grandfather)
John Brookes – 1821 (father)
William Brookes – 1851 (son)

This does appear to indicate (given approximately twenty-five years between fathers and sons) that the Cooper's Hill Wake was certainly happening, at the latest, by the mid-1700s. A report of the event in *The Gloucester Journal* of 13 June 1908 said:

> The principle thing of this ancient festival is of course the bowling of the cheese and amongst those present or immediately after this commenced on Monday were the Revd J.H. Seabrook, Mr S. Aitkin, Mr Dyer-Edwards, Mr Sheffield Blakeway, Mr Franklin Higgs, Mr and Mrs W.J. Thorpe, Mr T. Thorpe, Mr Scoball, Mr and Mrs James Fielding, Mr H.Y. Jones. Master of Ceremonies, Mr William Brookes. The latter is whom strangers see at this function always bedecked in a grey tall hat with a band or bands of red, white and blue and with a tail of many ribbons and a brilliant white smock with a bright flower in front. At all events that is how he appeared on Monday. As soon as he gets on the ground he starts to get things in order. The new pole is 60 feet high and was presented by Mr Dyer-Edwards from whose land it was cut. 6 cheeses in all were bowled.
>
> In addition to the cheese bowling there were numerous attractions which included a programme of children's sports and scrambling for buns.

1910

Another report from *The Gloucester Journal*, 21 May 1910:

> BROCKWORTH
> The wake was held on Cooper's Hill on Whit Monday as usual, but in consequence of heavy thunderstorms the number were actually few compared with other years, it actually pouring with rain up to the moment the proceedings were timed to commence. There were 5 cheeses sent down the hill, which were bowled by the following: Revd J.H. Seabrook, Miss Ethel Priday, Miss Jones, Mr H.Y. Jones.
>
> This year an innovation was introduced by Commander J.H. Jones R.N. who gave and rolled a cheese on a slight incline on the top of the hill, for the village maidens to run for. (This seems to have been the first ladies' race).
>
> The usual tug of war ladies v. gentlemen was captained by Miss Priday and Revd J.H. Seabrook respectively and resulted after a very continued struggle and amidst great applause with a win for the former. Other races took place and there were the usual coconut shys etc. on the summit of the hill. Mr William Brookes as usual, successfully carried out the duties of M.C. and his genial personality contributed largely to the success of the gathering.

1912

The following report appeared in *The Gloucestershire Echo*:

> 28 May 1912
> All roads along the countryside led on Whit Monday to Cooper's hill for the celebrated wake. With centuries behind it, this popular festival, which must not be confused with an Irish wake

'An ancient Gloucester Festival', 5 June 1911.

has in recent years had a decided 'revival' owing to the electric tram service having brought the hill within easy walking distance of Gloucestrians and also because of the determination of the parishioners of Brockworth to make the wake an annual demonstration against any infringement by the freeholders with their rights of common on the hill.

Favoured by beautiful weather on Monday the wake was even more largely attended than in late years. Among the company were: The Revd J. Herbert Seabrook (vicar of Brockworth), Mr William Priday J.P., Miss Ethel Priday, Mr Lawrence Priday, Mr Howard Abell, Mr and Mrs Y. Jones, Mr and Mrs Fitzgerald Jones, Commander Jones R.N., Major and Mrs Organ, City Councillor Colwell, Mr and Mrs Fenton, Mr Nott. Mr, Mrs and the Misses Holbrook, Mr and Mrs Walter Denton, Mr and Mrs Jarett Thorpe, Mr and Mrs Roland Austin, Mr Higgs (China Consular Service), Revd J.H. Jones, Mr Stafford Herbert etc.

Just on the stroke of 6 o'clock Mr William Brookes, full of 30 years continuous service as Master of Ceremonies began to assert his office. (William Brookes became M.C. in 1884).

Wearing as usual a brown top hat decked with variegated ribbons, which his father and mother won in a dancing contest in days of yore, and a chemise over his coat he stood by the maypole and repeatedly called to the crowd to form the 'alley' down the precipice (having a drop of quite one foot in two).

The course being clear, the vicar opened the ball by sending the first cheese (a disc of wood wrapped in pink paper) downhill. Helter skelter ran nine young men after it and most of them pitch-polled.

The first to secure the disc, stopped at the bottom by a hedge, had to trudge uphill again and there exchange it for the prize cheese. This bowling was repeated at intervals six times.

On one occasion the disc bounded, shortly after it had left a lady's hands and struck in the face two little girls standing on one side of the 'alley', but beyond being bruised they were not injured. Another cheese rounded? [this word is un-readable in the newspaper article] spectators at the foot by jumping into thick brambles and a search in which a few ubiquitous Boy Scouts took part, brought it to light.

A further instance of the dangerous nature of the activity was the falling down on it of a Gloucester boy and a few ribs were supposed to be broken thereby. Mr Fenton took him off at once in his motor car to the infirmary where an examination by three surgeons proved that he was not much hurt.

The cheese bowling was varied by some rural sports on a stretch of flat ground by the maypole. This included running, jumping in sacks and a tug-of-war in which the lady contestants once more pulled stronger than the mere men.

Some concomitants of a country fair were there for patronage, even in the form of a 'character reader' wearing gown and college cap.

The wake has taken a new lease of life and with better organisation it might be made even more attractive than in its present unconventional form.

1929

The following report appeared in *The Gloucestershire Echo*:

An amusing incident occurred in connection with the cheese. It was a rule that no competitor should in his pursuit climb any hedge.

The necessity for this was in fact completely eliminated since the disc representing the cheese bounded over the opposite hedge into the roadway where it was finally captured.

The following report appeared in *The Field*:

ROLLING THE CHEESES – An Old-Time Gloucestershire Custom by R. Clarkson Dixon.

At Cooper's Hill, four miles from the little stone-built town of Painswick and five miles from the county town of Gloucester, cheese are bowled down the hill every Whit-Monday. They are chased by the lads – and the lasses, too – of the village, who run helter-skelter down the hill, regardless of the possible damage to skin or bone.

The occasion is what is locally known as Cooper's Hill Wake, and it is one of the few surviving Cotswold customs. It is, of course, the gala-day of the year for the village, but although sports and different races are held after the Cheese Rolling, it is this which is the chief item on the programme, and which attracts to the hill thousands of visitors from the surrounding towns and villages.

Farmer William Brooks, Master of the Wake, is the most important man at Cooper's Hill on Whit-Monday, for it is he who lines up the lads of the village in a row at the top of the hill, and sends the big round cheese away down the hill. He is a happy old man, with always a smile on his face, a true son of the Cotswolds, possessing a wonderful personality.

On these occasions, old William Brooks is adorned with a white smock and a white top hat festooned with brightly-coloured ribbons. He always refers to his smock as his 'chemise', which is invariably washed the day following the Cheese Rolling and carefully put away until the next year. William is much older than he looks (he would have been 78 at that time). Indeed, he is reputed to be as old as the Wake itself, and certainly there is no-one who can remember anyone else but he holding the official title of 'Master of the Wake'. In spite of his great age he is gay and full of fun.' (As 'Master' from 1884, William had held the title for 45 years, and continued until his death in 1934 – a total of 50 years.)

'With a 'One – Two – Three – Go !' from William Brooks, away runs the cheese and away run the boys and girls, but faster still speeds the cheese, and very seldom is it captured before reaching the bottom of the hill. Generally the lucky (?) winner, who, in addition to retaining the cheese, receives as a prize the sum of two or three shillings, goes crashing through the hedge at the foot of the hill – cheese, or what is left of it – as well!

The cheese suffers rather badly during its career down the hill – Cooper's Hill is about a quarter of a mile in length – and bits of it fly off at angles as it hits stone after stone. The winner may consider himself very fortunate if he is able to retain a piece weighing more than a pound or so.

Of late years the cheese has been substituted by an imitation one, but there is always a real cheese waiting for the winner.

So what were they rolling? What 'bits' were flying off? What was the winner 'retaining'?

1937

Wednesday 12 May saw the Coronation of King George VI and on Friday 14 May, as part of the local Coronation celebrations, an unusual event took place. The headline in *The Citizen* read:

Torchlight Race up Cooper's Hill
A torch-light race from the foot of Cooper's Hill to the flagpole (maypole) at the top - reversing the famous Cheese Rolling race - finished Brockworth's Coronation Sports, and incidentally nearly finished some of the competitors.

Rejoicings began with a service at the Parish Church in the morning. In the afternoon, a programme of sports was held in a field adjoining the Robinson Memorial Hall (now the site of a house called 'Highways').

After tea the sports resumed, including 'bowling for a pig'.

The 'Empire Greeting Programme' and King's Speech were broadcast in the Hall in the evening and a torch-lit procession from the Hall to the foot of Cooper's Hill preceded the race.

At 10 o'clock the beacon was lighted. The general opinion was that it was one of the best bonfires seen on the hill.

[This was just three days before the Cheese Rolling of that year.]

1939–1945

Between the years 1939-1945 a substitute wooden cheese was used as food rationing was in force (see Chapter Five).

A government statement issued on 7 May 1941 gives context to this:

> The Ministry of Food said today that there was to be no general issue of cheese in catering establishments, only for residents of such establishments.

In 1940 the Whitsun bank holiday was cancelled because of the war. Although the Cheese Rolling did take place there was a smaller crowd than usual. This seems to have been the only year that was affected. On 4 June 1941, *The Citizen* headline said 'Carry on at Cooper's Hill'. It was the first time that real cheese was not used for the races and novelty races included a scramble for sweets. The Army had one race to themselves. The uphill races first took place during the late 1940s.

1946

By 1946 the committee was becoming concerned that car numbers were increasing, so a field was allocated for the purpose.

The following three photographs are thought to have been taken by Mr E. Tomkins apparently during the late 1930s:

Looking up the hill.

Spectators climbing the hill.

Crowds gather at the top of the hill.

1949

The following account appeared on Tuesday 7 June 1949 in *The Citizen*:

THRILLS AT COOPER'S HILL – WINNER GAINS HIS TENTH CHEESE

Once again the traditional Whitsun Cheese Rolling and Wake at Cooper's Hill, Brockworth, drew large crowds of spectators yesterday, and again they saw 22 years old rugby player Roy Mitchell win the first cheese event (his tenth cheese) and maintain his record of making the descent without a fall.

An hour before the first cheese was rolled, Cooper's Hill looked like a gigantic ant-hill, a moving crowd swarmed over the steep one-in-one gradient, and cars moved in a long line steadily up the narrow lane which leads to the base of the hill, while from all directions scattered groups of people on foot came to witness this age-old custom of Gloucestershire.

A bright array of summer dresses splashed colour on the hill-side and numbers of children scrambled up and down the slope, gleefully licking ice-creams – bought from a barrow which was doing a roaring trade on the warmest afternoon of the Whitsun holiday.

The master of ceremonies, Mr Tom Window, with a buttonhole as big as a bride's bouquet, had brought out his top-hat decked with red, white and blue ribbons and his customary white coat. He presided at the top of the hill, organised the children's race, which filled the programme between the Cheese Rolling events, and gave the 'away' to the competitors.

Up at the crest of the hill by the 50ft. maypole, traditionally topped with gorse and a weather-cock, three contestants lined up for the first 'roll' – and Mrs Hicks Beach sent the cheese bounding downwards. While the people held their breath the three men plunged. Roy Mitchell, who lives at the foot of the hill, made another sure-footed descent to win his tenth cheese.

The second cheese, rolled by Dr H. Lowry, was chased by another three competitors and won by J. Binder.

Perhaps the most breath-taking race was for the third cheese, rolled by the Revd de Lacy Mann, when a field of six girls entered.

Two of them bounced and somersaulted three-quarters of the way down and the ambulance brigade thought they had some customers, but Betty Hunt, bruised and smiling, was the first to reach the coveted cheese and no-one was hurt.

Bernard Morgan won the last cheese, rolled by Col. Thompson, beating four other boys in the field.

The uphill race had the most entrants of the events and spectators were thrilled when a small girl in a blue dress went leaping ahead of a crowd of boys, but she hadn't the 'staying power' and flagged on the last lengths, and the race was won by T. Brewster.

A tug of war was held at the top of the hill in an interval.

The organisation of the event was by a committee which included Mr W. Jones (chairman), Mrs J. Hall, Mrs G. Buckle and Messrs. L.T. Millard, A. Gregory, H.W .Mitchell, C.R. Stephens, J.E. Morgan, C.W.Yates and Tom Windo.

A parking charge was introduced of 1s per car and 6d per motorcycle.

1951

It was reported either in *The Citizen* or *The Gloucester Journal* that:

> The third race was for women. No woman – young or old – would step forward. So three Brockworth Girl Guides volunteered.
>
> They waited tensely on the hill-top for Mr J.P. Burroughs to roll the mock-cheese. The hundreds cheered as the three small figures tumbled to the bottom.
>
> Thirteen-years-old Jean MacDonald somersaulted a dozen times on the last hill-side hillock and fell into the judge's arms to earn her ten-shilling note.

1952

On 2 June 1952 a headline in *The Citizen* read:

> Cheese Rolling May Be On T.V.
>
> BBC tele-cameramen from London recorded the tumbling, slips and half-dives of the competitors as they raced down the slope after the elusive five-pound wooden cheese (now used instead of the usual seven-pounder cheese).

1957

In 1957 *The Citizen* reported that a young boy was burnt as he 'bowled down the hill' with a box of matches in his pocket. The matches burst into flames. It seems that he was not taking part in a race at the time.

Until 1959 the costs incurred in upholding the annual Cheese Rolling and Wake were met from subscriptions of local residents. The number of vehicles parking for the event was however increasing and the owners of the fields used agreed to donate the takings to the Wake. Residents' subscriptions are not mentioned after this date.

1966

The parking charge was increased to 2s per car, the first increase since 1949.

1967

The date was again changed from the Church's Whit Monday to the National Spring bank holiday Monday.

1971

Currency became decimalised and car parking cost 30p.

1981

Car parking increased to 50p. The author of the following account is unknown:

> Not many years ago, the pole used to be decorated with flowers, ribbon and gorse (some authorities say it was painted too) every Whit-Monday but unfortunately this lapsed.
>
> The scattering of sweets and buns, which may have symbolised the fruits of the coming harvest, especially when the event was held in mid-summer, has also lapsed.
>
> The whole custom of Cooper's Hill Wake and the once annual erection of the maypole is supposed to maintain the grazing rights of the Commoners of Cooper's Hill.
>
> The Cooper's Hill Wake was quite an elaborate affair.
> Over the years, the event has been given publicity by radio and television and has attracted visitors from home and overseas.
>
> During the late 1970s the event was threatened by the erosion and rutting of the slope face, caused by people climbing the slope during the year. The slope was fenced for a year and gladly, there was no break in the tradition of holding the annual event.
>
> The continuation of the Cheese Roll is not guaranteed by a national body, but by the desire of local people and a committee of local residents to continue the ceremony.
>
> There are no admission charges, money is raised from the car parking to pay for cheeses.
>
> An annual collection is made in aid of charity.

Two Ghurkha soldiers, Kul Bahadur Gurung and Pretap Limbu serving with the 6th and 7th Rifle Regiments stationed at Sandhurst, took part in the chase. Their Company Major Patrick Davis lived at Well Close on Cooper's Hill.

1982

Monday 31 May 1982 was a hot, sunny day. It seemed an ideal day for the annual Cheese Rolling on Cooper's Hill. This was obviously the opinion of hundreds of people who climbed the hill. Just after the first race of the evening the storm began with hail, thunder and lightning. Some people instinctively ran for cover under nearby trees. Unfortunately trees can be hazardous in a storm and two families were struck by lightning. Eight people (including four children) were taken to hospital. They were Mr Paul Curtis, his wife Helen and their six-year-old son Craig, Mr Alan Smedley, his wife Barbara, twin sons Stephen and Gareth aged seven, and Adele aged six. Only Paul Curtis was detained in hospital overnight with bruising to his back.

The Citizen reported:

> Mr Smedley said, 'We were standing in a field below the hill because it was a better view for the children. We saw the first race and after that it started to hammer down. Against our better judgement we did the natural thing and ran for cover under trees. They were sheltering under the tree with Mr Curtis and his family when lightning struck. I didn't hear or see anything, just a crackling sound. One minute we were standing there, the next minute we weren't. The next thing I can really remember is being on the ground about five yards away with a mass of bodies everywhere. The worst thing was not being able to move – I was paralysed. I was kneeling on the ground and I just didn't have the legs to stand up. We should have known better than to go under a tree, but it always happens to someone else doesn't it?'

Only the stalwarts remained on the hill after the storm to see the remaining competitors run, slip and slide in quick succession down the hill before they slithered and paddled their way home.

1986

At a meeting held by Gloucestershire County Council's Recreation and Leisure Committee bylaws were called for to protect the hill. However it was not realised they would stop things like Cheese Rolling and blackberry picking. The county solicitor was asked to look at the proposals.

The cost of car parking was increased to £1.

1989

In May several papers (*The Sunday Mirror, The Daily Star* and *The Independent*) reported how a cheese had injured a child, 'causing severe back injuries' during the Cheese Roll that week. It happened when a cheese hit an irregularity in the hill and veered off into the crowd. Two children were taken to hospital: Laura Carpenter, aged eight, was hit in the back by a cheese but was allowed home after treatment; Simon Roberts, also eight years old, suffered cuts to his head and leg when one of the runners fell and collided with him. Simon too went home after treatment.

The ground surface is very uneven and warnings are constantly given to the public over the public address system about the danger of the unpredictability of the path of the cheese. People are asked to watch each cheese so that they can take avoiding action if necessary and to keep a close watch on their children for that reason.

1997

The Cheese Roll was again held on the annual spring bank holiday. Several thousand spectators were there as well as many fearless contenders for the cheeses. The media was present in force, including cameras from BBC, HTV, ITV and a freelance cameraman who was syndicating to countries worldwide. (I received a message from Atlanta, USA the following day to say that the event had featured in their news broadcast!). Unfortunately that year, modern times caught up with the tradition and two cheeses were stolen before injured winners could claim them.

1998

1998 really deserves its own chapter! The police had been very concerned by the number of injuries (most of them fairly minor) that were reported the previous year. The following statement was issued to the press on Tuesday 19 May, (the week before the bank holiday) by the Cheese Roll Committee:

> The organising committee of the Cooper's Hill Cheese Rolling has reluctantly concluded that because of bureaucratic constraints related to public safety, the great spectacle of the Cheese Rolling cannot take place this year.
>
> Adverse and inappropriate comments recently seen in the local press have precipitated reaction from those in charge of essential services that attend the Cheese Rolling. This has resulted in preconditions being set that in the view of the Committee cannot be guaranteed.
>
> The safety of the public has always been of paramount importance to the organisers and because of the inherent risks associated with the event the Committee has made its reluctant decision.

Dancing in the rain in 1982. (*The Citizen*)

Wet! 1982. (*The Citizen*)

The Committee's intentions are to ensure that the long-standing tradition of Cheese Rolling will be continued and will remain a part of the culture of Gloucestershire.

The landowners of Cooper's Hill had become increasingly concerned about public liability, a view possibly not helped by exaggerated reports of injuries.

St John's Ambulance Service had always been willing to treat any injuries as they occurred, but were no longer able to climb the hill to help. In recent years a cave rescue team had helped in this respect. Unfortunately the committee was unable to secure the services of the cave-rescue team this time, and reluctantly cancelled the event six days before the Wake was due to take place.

The committee and local residents however, were determined that there should not be a break in the tradition. After lengthy research it seems unlikely that a break has ever occurred before. At 6.30a.m. on the bank holiday Monday, about twenty people gathered on the hill to perpetuate the Cheese Rolling.

Just one cheese was rolled by a local resident, Mrs Liz Davis, and it was 'chased', rather sedately, by a handful of people.

Peter Astman was the first man to reach the bottom (both his mother and father won races in 1943) and Amelia Hardwick, aged eight years, was the first lady.

Traditionally the winners of the races keep the cheese as their prize. As there was only one race on this occasion and therefore only one cheese, it had been decided that the cheese would be shared between the people who were present at this historic event. So after a ceremonial cutting of the cheese using a Ghurkha kukri knife that had belonged to the late Maj. Patrick Davis, the assembled company went home to enjoy a cheese breakfast secure in the knowledge that the ancient custom of Cheese Rolling had not been allowed to die. Of course there were reactions to the cancelling of the Cheese Rolling and Wake of 1998. Reporters and photographers arrived too late to see any action and had to buy photographs of the early-morning run. The event did not go unrecorded in the press and the following headline examples indicate the local and national interest:

Under cover of dark they crept out for an illicit cheese roll on the hill
   The Daily Telegraph

Cheese rolls on the early morning menu
   The Western Daily Press

Cheese Rolling Called Off
   The Citizen

Cheese tradition rolls to an end
   The Times

Who cut the cheese?
   The Guardian

The BBC made a statement on Ceefax about the day's happenings. It read:

A token Cheese Rolling ceremony has taken place in Gloucestershire, to replace the cancelled public event. This afternoon's spectacle was cancelled amid public safety fears. But about 30 cheese

Above and below: Photographs taken in 1991 and 1992 show how difficult it is for competitor to remain on their feet during a downhill race. (Jean Jefferies)

The unthinkable! (Jean Jefferies)

rollers met at first light to ensure that the tradition – which stretches back centuries – remained unbroken. Organisers say that the public Cheese Rolling should be re-instated next year.

It was certainly a day to remember for the residents of Cooper's Hill!

1999

Another year to remember. Following the cancellation of the public event of 1998 because of 'bureaucratic constraints related to public safety', new safety measures were employed. After a great deal of hard work by committee members the undergrowth down the edges of the slope was severely cut back, lower tree branches were taken off (by commoners who have that right), and orange sheep fencing was put down the length of the slope. This was to keep spectators away from the face and help to protect them from any stray cheeses that might go off course. Stewards were employed to help with crowd control and a private medical team (including a doctor) were present to act as back up for St John's Ambulance personnel who were on duty. A mountain rescue team was there to help move any casualties from the face of the hill.

The crowd flocked to the top …. (Jean Jefferies)

…. and the foot of the hill to see the race. (Jean Jefferies)

Sign announcing change of start time. (Jean Jefferies)

Another big decision was taken to move the event from its usual starting time of 6 p.m. in the evening to midday. The effects of alcohol on those taking part is not a recent problem. 'Fighting and ruffianism' were reported as far back as 1890 but it was argued that by holding the event earlier in the day this would give those present on the hill less drinking time before the event and would consequently avoid any difficult confrontation. The day was a tremendous success! The crowds were not as great as usual but this was probably as a result of the dull weather. The fences not only gave the spectators a boundary, they also enabled the stewards to help limit the number of entrants in each race. This was accepted in good spirit and caused no problems. All injuries were minor and all contestants went home under their own steam. There was a real family atmosphere, everyone seemed to enjoy themselves and there was no trouble. Of course these added measures greatly increased the cost of staging the event. The costs are met only from car park charges so inevitably these had to be raised. Parking a car increased from £1 to £5 and motorbikes to £2.50. The last increase was in 1986.

There were more news headlines to follow:

It will be a welcome return
The Citizen

Gentlemen, Start Your Cheeses: Historic Race Returns to England
The Wall Street Journal

English countryside ripe for cheese rolling
The Japan Times

Cheese rolls back on the menu
Gloucestershire Echo

Cheesy grins for the high rollers
The Daily Telegraph

Cheese roll leaves the competition stumbling
The Times

Cheese chase is on a roll again
The Citizen

The maypole, which was found on the ground on 9 March 1999, had not been replaced by the time of the Wake. This is possibly the first time that the Cheese Rolling has taken place without a maypole.

2000

The maypole was re-erected during the year. Unfortunately it was not replaced with a new, full-sized pole. Instead the one that was pushed over during the previous year had its base trimmed and it was re-erected as a truncated version of its former self. The cockerel that had been found nailed to a farm fence earlier in the year was replaced on top of the pole shortly before Cheese Roll day.

The committee's arrangements for the year were similar to those for 1999. Stewards were once more employed to assist with crowd control and the private medical team was present as well as a team from St John's Ambulance Brigade, to attend to any injuries that might occur. An innovation was the provision of a compound for the members of the press and television crews. This was a fenced area at the foot of the hill to give them protection equal to that given to the spectators. This seemed to give all the media people not only the safety intended but also a base for interviews with winners and an uninterrupted view of the events.

2001

The next three years were rather unusual in the life of the Cheese Rolling. In the spring of 2001 there was an outbreak of foot-and-mouth disease among cattle in the UK, and movement of all farm animals was restricted.

Public footpaths were closed and the Cheese Rolling that was due to take place on 28 May was cancelled, possibly for the first time in its history. (The event had been stopped officially for security reasons in 1998 but the committee had run a single token race early in the morning.) This time, even the committee, who remain dedicated to keeping the Cheese Rolling tradition alive, felt quite unable to run even a token race on the day. Local inhabitants stopped using the hill and surrounding areas, even for dog walking, so a gathering for maintaining the ancient tradition was quite out of the question. However on 31 July when the emergency was over, a group of local residents rolled one cheese and once more maintained the ancient tradition.

2002

The year of the Queen's Jubilee. It was fifty years since Queen Elizabeth had succeeded to the throne and many celebrations were to take place throughout Britain on the May bank holiday Monday. The committee therefore decided to hold the Cheese Rolling and Wake the following day, possibly the first time cheeses had been rolled on a Tuesday. There were considerably fewer spectators than usual and car-park takings were down.

2003

Plans were going well and the cheeses had been ordered and delivered when disaster struck – not in Gloucestershire but in Algeria. During the last week of May 2003, there was a significant earthquake in Northern Algeria which was to affect the cheese rolling. As mentioned before, the event is attended each year by members of St John's Ambulance. They are present to deal with any casualties that occur during the day. They are, however, not insured to help anyone who is injured on the slope so they rely on a search and rescue team, Rapid UK, to help casualties off the hill.

Rapid UK had been called to help in Algeria so, at the last minute on Friday afternoon, three days before Cheese Rolling, St John's Ambulance had to withdraw their help for Monday. Without medical and rescue cover, the Cheese Rolling and Wake of 2003 had to be cancelled. Messages were put out on internet, local radio and press but it was too late to inform many spectators, particularly the international media who were already on their way! A group of people from the area who knew about the cancellation had organised themselves to keep the tradition going. Large numbers of people still arrived and there was traffic chaos on the single-track lane. The members of the committee could not be involved (for insurance reasons) so there was no field open for the usual car parking.

They had great fun chasing a yellow ball down the hill. There were no reports of any injuries. One cheese was rolled by the committee the following week, once more continuing the tradition. The cheeses that had already been ordered and delivered by the time the event was cancelled were sold for charity.

Above: The orange sheep fencing can be seen down the side of the hill to protect and control the spectators. This is erected and all other preparations are undertaken by the committee members before the event each year. (Jean Jefferies)

Left: Steve Brain, the 1999 champion, was interviewed by the press at the foot of the hill. The straw bales behind him are for the safety of the competitors as they hurtle down the hill. Although there are proficient rugby-tackling catchers at the end of the race, the bales form extra protection from a high-speed crash into the boundary hedge and fence. (Jean Jefferies)

Above and below: The eventual winner of all three races that year, Steve Brain, is the only man still on his feet. (Chris Ison)

Straw bales to protect out of control runners from the metal fence posts and fencing. (Jean Jefferies)

2004

In 2004 everything went according to plan. The crowds were bigger than ever. Several television teams came from abroad. A Belgian company had persuaded one of their football heroes to run in one of the races. He had agreed before seeing the hill! Marc Ellis, a New Zealand All Black rugby player was a winner of one of the cheeses, and another New Zealander, Dionne Carter won the ladies' race. There was also a battle of the giants.

Stephen Gyde and Steven Brain were old adversaries. Stephen Gyde was the winner of twenty-one cheeses in fourteen years (1976-1993) and Steven Brain won seventeen cheeses in sixteen years. In five of those years (1984, 1986, 1987, 1988 and 1990) they both won cheeses. 2004 was comeback year for them both. The two of them entered the first race.

2005

The hill had been well prepared by members of the committee the previous day.

This was the busiest year yet! There were about 1,000 cars in the car park and probably about 5,000 people on the hill. There was a television crew from the children's programme *Blue Peter*, one from Canada and many others.

Above and below: The protective compound for members of the media. (Sue Burn)

Above: Men's races in 2000 – downhill and …. (E. Ashenden)

Below: … uphill. (E. Ashenden)

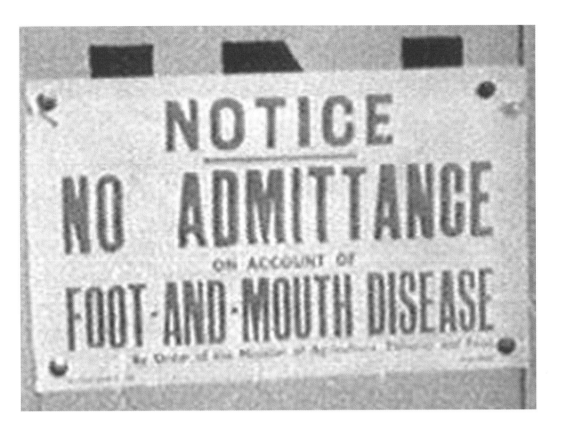

Above and right: Notices appeared in and around Gloucester as the epidemic grew. (Jean Jefferies)

Cheese Rollers
DO NOT DESPAIR!
THE MEDICS ARE IN
ALGERIA ... BUT
THE HILLS STILL
THERE ...
Coopers Hill
MON 26th May
11.00 AM

Above: Local residents at the unofficial Cheese Roll in 2001. (Jean Jefferies)

Left: Steven Brain is at the front, going well. Stephen Gyde (wearing a white vest) has already lost his footing! Seconds after the photo was taken disaster struck Steven Brain. He fell, probably caught his foot in a hole, and broke his ankle. Stephen Gyde, however, continued gently down the hill and was delighted to come third. (Jean Jefferies)

High fencing will stop the 70mph flying cheese before it hits the cottage. (Jean Jefferies)

2006

The month of May had above average rainfall. Conditions had been so bad that messages were given out by local radio suggesting that visitors either park away from the hill or stay away altogether. On the Thursday before the event a photograph of the extremely muddy entrance to the car park (normally a cattle field) was put on the website www.cheese-rolling.co.uk and people were asked to bring their wellies or walking boots.

Local people were very concerned about the conditions. The forecast was for rain. However, high winds during the weekend dried the ground quite well although the going was still soft. Monday dawned bright and sunny but just as the first cheese rolled on its way – down came the rain!

But nothing would dampen the enthusiasm of the competitors as they ran, tumbled and slid down the hill after the cheese. For the runners mud was the order of the day!

The showers that seemed to time themselves for each race were quite heavy and there was even hail. In between the showers the sun was hot and umbrellas were up and down all day. The soft going did mean that injuries were few as sliding was the easiest way to come down. There was an extra downhill race introduced for men to give the ever rising number of competitors a chance to join in. There were four uphill races, one each for boys under twelve, girls under twelve, men and women.

Left: Fencing down the sides of the hill are erected for crowd safety. (Jean Jefferies)

Below: Farmer and chairman, Tony Pither, brings straw bales for 'crash barrier' at the foot of the hill. (Jean Jefferies)

Right and below: Paramedics from St John's Ambulance were ready as were the team from SARAID (Search and Rescue in Disasters) who were there to move any casualties from the hill. (Jean Jefferies)

More work at the site. (Jean Jefferies)

three

Masters of Ceremonies

The Master of Ceremonies (MC) traditionally wore a white smock and a top hat decorated with coloured ribbons, and he carried a staff. He also wore a buttonhole of red, white and blue flowers. These included a red peony, white lilies of the valley and blue cornflowers picked from the garden of Brookes Cottage on the hill. Nothing has changed except the smock or *chemise*. This sadly became too worn to repair and at some time in Tom Windo's reign (1934-1955) it was replaced by a modern farmer's white overall. The MC has the task of organising and starting the races. He is in charge at the top of the hill and decides who should be in a race and gives the instructions:

> ONE to be ready
> TWO to be steady
> THREE to prepare … at which point the guest roller sends the cheese away
> FOUR to be off … and the competitors hurl themselves down the precipice

At the time of writing, six MCs have been identified. They are:

Thomas Organ

According to H.Y.J. Taylor writing in 1890 of his earliest recollections, Mr Organ, 'a fine, tall, handsome fellow' was Master of Ceremonies. This could be around 1830-1840. The 1841 census shows that Thomas Organ was a resident of Cooper's Hill – perhaps he was the MC at that time. In 1870, Mr W.R. Organ claimed to have followed the cheese when he was 'a lad of 17'.

Mr William Brookes 1884-1934

Mr William Brookes was MC from 1884 until he died in October 1934, at the age of eighty-three. He had been an employee of the Midland Railway and walked daily from where he resided at Brookes Cottage near the foot of the Cheese Roll hill to work in Gloucester. He left home at 4 a.m. to be at work for 6 a.m., and arrived home in the evening at 8 p.m. or later. Traditionally, the button-hole of flowers worn by the MC is picked from the garden of Brookes Cottage. In 1934, Tom Windo and H. Gregory officiated jointly. Bill Brookes died in October of that year.

Tom Windo 1934-1955

Tom Windo was born in 1879 and worked at Cooper's Hill quarries. He succeeded Mr William Brookes as MC in 1934 and retired in 1955. He is said to have 'chased the cheese' himself in his youth and was obviously a great local character. It was during Tom Windo's reign as MC that the traditional smock worn for years at the Wake finally became irreparable. After much discussion, it was decided to move on a stage and replace it with a white overall as worn by farmers of the day.

Mr Edward (Ted) Millard 1958-1973

Ted Millard was a farmer living at Well Close Farm on Cooper's Hill. He was a skilled hedger and rick thatcher and a very knowledgeable countryman. By making careful observations of changes in nature he was able to forecast weather with great accuracy.

Mr Arthur Bick 1973-1989

In 1978 Mr Arthur Bick was unable to officiate as MC as he injured a hip falling off a ladder. Mr Bill Cooper took his place.

Mr Rob Seex 1990-present

The MC traditionally carries a wooden staff while carrying out his duties.
  Rob Seex has cut a notch on his for each event when he has officiated with a crossed notch for each of the three years when the public event has been cancelled.

Above, left and right: Tom Windo 1934. (Gloucester Folk Museum)

Bill Brookes. (Gloucester Folk Museum)

Detail on the back of the old smock. (Eric Tomkins)

Above left: Ted Millard.

Above right: Mr Arthur Bick 1973-1989. (William Organ)

Left: Rob Seex became Master of Ceremonies on the death of Arthur Bick in 1990. (Jeremy Kaye)

four

Quotes and Personalities

At Home

Watch the cheese all the way down and be prepared to move!

This was the constant warning given out over the public address system by Tony Peasley, the long-serving commentator and spokesman for the Cheese Roll. He was involved with Cheese Rolling for forty-six years until his death in 2002.

1903

Tom Windo, who was born in 1879 within sight of Cooper's Hill and who later became Master of Ceremonies, took a severe tumble himself when chasing the cheese in 1903. He was off work for a week. He said, 'In those days we used to go round to all the farms, getting cider, and then sing and dance on the hill all night and sometimes next day.'

1901 or 1911

The source of this article is unknown and the date is most likely to be 1911 and was written by Miss M.M. Godfrey of The Greenway, Shurdington:

WHITSUNTIDE SPORTS AT COOPER'S HILL
These games have taken place on Whit-Monday for over two hundred years. Though now shorn of their former glory, some of the old customs are carried out. The Master of the Ceremonies has a peculiar dress for the occasion – a white top-hat, this year decorated with Coronation ribbons, and a woman's smock which is worn over his coat, and consequently has to be of huge dimensions. Said smock is raced for at the end of the evening by women.

This photograph was taken 'One Whit Monday, just after the First World War'. It was kindly lent by Roy Mitchell whose family lived on the hill. He was a great competitor in the 1940s and won ten cheeses over eight years. On the back of the photograph is a description of the presentation of a pork pie to Bill Brookes, possibly as a gift in recognition of his duties. No other reference to this has been found. From left to right: Mr Priday JP of Hucclecote, Mrs Priday, Bill Brookes, (unknown boy behind), Bert Leech of Green Lane, Miss Ethel Priday. Ethel Priday later became chairman of the Cheese Roll Committee and served for many years until her death in 1947.

The chief sport now is the rolling of three or four cheeses down a steep part of the hill, which cheeses the men and boys race for.

It appears to strangers to be a most dangerous game, but the hill people appear quite unconcerned.

The present Master of the Ceremonies, William Brookes tells me that he can remember when country dances of an intricate nature were danced on the top of the hill, and when ribbons were given as prizes. He showed me one that his mother had danced for.

Boys would grin through a horse-collar, and the ugliest face got a prize, and all sorts of good-humoured horse-play went on. But the 'old order changeth.' The cyclist day has dawned. People can go far afield now for amusement, and rustic sports are no longer the only amusement open to a village.

Even now the Cooper's Hill games attracted a great number of people, and I took this photograph (unfortunately not found) in fear of being pushed down the hill with the cheeses by the pressure of the excited crowd.

In these days of modern transport, and the resulting congestion and parking problems, it is amusing to realise that the coming of the bicycle should increase the numbers of people coming to see the Cheese Rolling and Wake.

1937

Bert Gregory:

There's a knack in this game all right. The main thing is to get well off at the start and keep your footing. It's not like the old days. Jim Twinning was talking to me just now and we both agreed that we could beat this lot. They used to put me back on scratch, handicap me, but even then I used to get away so that I was almost up to the cheese.

They used to roll as many as nine or ten cheeses. That was before the War (1914-18). I do not think I ran after the War. I am 57 now and even in those days I was getting a bit stiff. It jolly well shakes you up coming down here.

No, I never broke any bones at it, but I have had gravel-rash and the sole of my boot cut off as if it had been done by a knife. I know this hill like the back of my hand, because I have lived here all my life.

The pole (may-pole) used to be taken down and freshly painted for the event. Farmers all round the district used to give jars of cider and there was free beer too. Things were much more lively up top here then, I can tell you.

I can remember winning as many as six cheeses in an evening.

Bert Gregory chased cheeses for more than a quarter of a century and at that time had won more than any other man in the district with the possible exception of Jim Twinning of Cheltenham. He was the nephew of the late Mr William Brookes who once lived in Brookes Cottage, Cooper's Hill and was MC at the Cooper's Hill Wake for half a century. At this time Bert Gregory was living in Brookes Cottage.

1938

So long as there are people anxious to clamber up Cooper's Hill to enjoy this truly British good fun, there are young folk ready to rush downwards above a perfect English landscape, no man will have cause to say that Gloucestershire has lost itself in a machine age.

C.G.T., possibly writing in *The Citizen* or *The Gloucester Journal*.

1939

Mr J. Lord said that he had been attending for about thirty years (since about 1909) and remembered there being sellers of sweets and gingerbread at the event.

1942

Local resident Rosemary Hellerman (née Smart and later Mrs Astman), present owner of the nearby Haven Tea Garden, then aged seventeen, ran in a race on a very wet day. Few people had entered the race and, wearing her school mac and wellingtons, Rosemary won her cheese! As it was wartime the cheese was wooden so the prize was £1. She said:

Then I had to climb all the way back up the hill with the cheese because it was needed for the last race!

In 1976 she rolled a real cheese.

In his book *Gloucestershire* written in about the 1940s Kenneth Hare suggests that:

Trainers of Commandos in search of novel strenuosities might do worse than visit Cooper's Hill, two miles from Birdlip Village, upon the occasion of the annual Cheese Rolling on Whit-Monday … I was given a tip by a knowing road-mender who formerly, in the teeth of the most furious competition, achieved the coveted prize.

'Wear spiked boots,' said he. 'Unless you wear spiked boots, there's no keeping your footing on they slopes. It bean't to be done.'

'Good,' thought I, 'until you set your heel upon the other fellow's uppers!'

'Will Cheese Rolling survive this second world war?'

'Of course!' chimes in a friendly hedger-and-ditcher, 'Us were Cheese Rolling bevore new-fangled vootball an' cricket were thought on!'

Kenneth Hare describes how:

The Master of Ceremonies, that sturdy old man, hospitably invited me into his cottage, and regaled me with a host of interesting and sometimes lurid details … My old M.C. shows me the uniform in which he officiates: his smock-frock. Surely his must be the last garment of this type throughout the length and breadth of England to be publicly worn. The front is ornamented with curious stitching, and dating, as it does, from that honest epoch before the politicians began to promise us, at our own expense, the last of their batch of brave new worlds, it still shows little trace of wear … Bill shows me his hat, which is not, as invariably reported, a 'topper', but a genuine white beaver contemporary with the smock … About the hatband, Bill has knotted six gay ribbons. 'One for each of my mourners,' says he, 'when I pass on: favours for remembrance.'

'Once', Bill tells me, 'long ago, a tragedy turned the mirth at one of these meetings into mourning. Whilst the young fellows chased the cheese, the young women were racing, upon the flat ground, for a smock. One light-heeled wench easily outdistanced all her fellows, caught the smock, flourished it about her head in triumph, and even as the cheering burst out, suddenly fell stone dead!'

'Today,' says Bill, 'the cheese is rolled, and ther'll be a tug-o'-war an' such, an' there be an end. But in my young days, every brewery for miles about sent us a barrelful FREE! So soon as the beer-wagon came in sight the fun began, and not one of us dreamed of leaving whilst a single drop o' that remained. After the cheese had been rolled, there were donkey races, and dancing and gallivanting; and the boys and girls never thought about going home until it were breakfast time the morning after. Happy days!'

1943

Minutes of committee meeting, 1 May:

It was agreed to invite the ambulance members to attend, also the Police, if latter think it their duty to do so.

1947

Ronald Beamish, who won two races that year said:

> We raced against some German Prisoners of War who were working in local factories at the time.

1948

Miss Dorothy Pearson from America rolled one of the cheeses. She was one of 124 schoolteachers who came to England for twelve months under an exchange scheme and was teaching at Denmark Road High School. She said of the Cooper's Hill ceremony:

> We have nothing like this in America, for we are not old enough to have such traditions. I shall certainly have something to tell the folks when I get back home.

1950

The Women's Institute published a booklet entitled *I Remember – Social Life in Gloucestershire Villages – 1850-1950*. Upton WI (close to Cooper's Hill) said of the Wake:

> After the Wake was over ruffianism commenced. Village feuds, grudges and personal quarrels were then settled. Hats were thrown in the air, rings were formed and sanguinary and prolonged fights followed.

Brockworth WI said:

> Cooper's Hill has always held a prominent part in the life of Brockworth (to whose parish the hill belongs) by virtue of its commanding position and its centuries-old Wake, held on Whit Monday, when the sport of cheese chasing down the precipitous slope takes place.

1951

Ice cream and lemonade vendors recorded record sales. Mr Arthur Kleinman said:

> I sold 1,000 packets of crisps and 20 gallons of lemonade. I had to send back for fresh supplies of water.

1952

A headline in *The Citizen* on Tuesday 2 June:

CHEESE ROLLING MAY BE ON TELEVISION
BBC tele-cameramen from London recorded the tumbling, slips and half-dives of the competitors as they raced down the slope after the elusive five-pound wooden cheese (now used instead of the seven-pounder cheese).

The festivities that have been taking place, possibly for centuries, on Cooper's Hill in deepest Gloucestershire, were now to be seen throughout the nation!

1955–1956

Rosemary Cooke, now living in British Columbia, Canada won three ladies' races and came second in another. She writes:

> I had watched boys race down Cooper's Hill for several years. I was brought up on a farm and a keen participant in sports and I felt I could do anything they could, so in 1953, at the reckless age of 16, I asked the announcer if we could have a ladies' race. He said we could if there were enough participants. About five girls answered his call and I was lucky enough to win … I climbed the hill with the cheese and they all cheered. The announcer made me wave to him. I won 10s.

In 1954 she was only second and won 5s. This being the first year when real cheese was reintroduced she was very disappointed not to come first and win a cheese. In 1955 however, she was again first and won a 30lb New Zealand Cheddar cheese. In the following year Rosemary won once more and took home a sprained ankle and an 8lb Caerphilly cheese. It seems that when the wooden cheese was used the winner had to return it to the top of the hill ready for the next race. In 1955 the newspaper report of Rosemary's win said, 'According to tradition, the winners should carry their cheeses to the top of the hill again, but a modern Sir Galahad came to Rosemary's aid, and carried her cheese up the hill'. There is no further mention of this tradition, which almost certainly started when the wooden cheese was used (during food rationing). There was only one dummy cheese which would have been needed at the top of the hill for each race.

1956

Peter Scott who rolled a cheese that year said:

> It looks frightening!

Peter Scott, later Sir Peter Scott, the son of Sir Robert Falcon Scott the Antarctic Explorer, was a well known naturalist, artist and broadcaster. He founded what is now known as the Wildfowl and Wetlands Trust at Slimbridge in Gloucestershire.

1976

Dave Allen, a well known Irish comedian, was a visitor to the Cheese Roll. He was present with a television crew filming for a programme about British people, legends, follies and customs. He said:

> It's the nearest thing to Kamikaze pilots I've ever seen!

1986

Arthur Bick said, on the origins of the cheese rolling:

> I should think that the landowners used to have a get-together once a year to test their ciders and cheese and the strength of their labour.

1987

At the end of the day, Superintendent Wingate of St John's Ambulance was pleased to report very few casualties:

> Cuts and bruises and a few strains – the usual sort of thing for this event.

1988

Rebecca Haines who had been stretchered off the previous year for x-rays to her head, said:

> I must have done something to my brain to do it again. I like cheese but a nine-pound one won't fit in our fridge at home!

1988 was also the year that BBC Television produced a programme about the Cheese Roll. Their 'ace reporter' (his words!) Chris Searle was doing a series about unusual events around the country called *Chris Searle's Summer Season*. He arrived on the morning of the Wake, with his own cheese (a Dutch Edam) in a bag to meet Arthur Bick who was MC at that time. They met in a field on the lower slopes of the hill. Arthur Bick rolled his cheese for him and Chris Searle chased after it. Having caught it he said that he didn't know what the fuss was all about! Later that day, when the real event was underway Chris joined in with a race. Having staggered down last and having suffered 'abrasions to the jeans', he declared that the hill was:

> Like the cliffs of Acapulco – vertical!

1991

In an interview with Pat Gawler, a student at Edinburgh University who was researching for her work *Custom and Today's Society*, Iris Peasley said:

> A child has two special days a year – its birthday and Christmas Day, but a child on Cooper's Hill has three days.

Mrs Iris Peasley and her family have been residents of the hill for generations – her Uncle Edward (Ted) Millard was MC between 1958-1973 and her father Len Millard was a committee member in the 1930s and 1940s.

1992

Winner Terry Sawczuk, having come second and third in past events, said:

That's been my ambition for years, but now I've finally done it - never again!

1993

Rob Preece who won two races said:

Your heart jumps as you fly over the top and there's no stopping after that!

Bill Jones said that a decorated cartwheel was once rolled, not a cheese. This suggests that the Cheese Rolling may go back to pagan days, when stones and wheels were rolled in sun worshipping rites at midsummer.

1994

It was reported in *The Citizen* that one year in the distant past, one spectator was actually killed by the cheese. The epitaph to the dead man read:

Here lies Billy, if you please,
Hit in the stomach with a cheese,
Cheese is wholesome fayre, they say,
It turned poor Billy into clay.

Also in 1994 an account was written by Mr G.J. Packer, a former resident of Witcombe over sixty years ago, now living in Ipswich, Queensland, Australia. Under the heading *Once Upon a Time* he reminisced about his life as a schoolboy and chorister at Witcombe and also about a Cheese Rolling experience:

I was also impressed by another event, reported, unfeelingly I thought, in the local newspaper of the day (about 1933): 'At Cooper's Hill, on Whit Monday, a small boy was struck by the cheese'. Whilst here, in Australia, one could be forgiven for thinking that a small boy had been slapped by his mother with the filling from a sandwich for being naughty or something, Witcombe and Brockworth folk would have known differently. I certainly did: I was that small boy – and that was some cheese! I was half-way down that hill, amongst the crowd, when this monstrous, wayward millstone, made of solid cheese, became airborne. I was collected by this errant lump of sour-cream, firmly moved down the hill,- a little boy flattened, knocked out, stood up, dusted off and pointed homewards, being carried for most of the way on my brother's back. Can you imagine that today? No doctor, no ambulance, no rescue helicopter, not even a bit of cheese! Why then do I not hate cheese? I love it!

1995

On Saturday 1 April, *The Citizen* reported:

> EU Threat to Cheese Chasers
> Gloucester's traditional spring bank holiday frolics at Cooper's Hill are under threat from new European Community food rulings.

The article went on to say:

> New hygiene rules meant that cheese could not change hands in the open air after being rolled on the ground. New rules would also prevent competitive games being held on slopes greater than 45 degrees, or 50% gradient in Eurospeak.

A special Cheese Roll hotline was given at the end of the article. On Monday, 3 April *The Citizen* admitted the April fool's joke. Apparently scores of people did phone in response to the article!
On May 30 the *Gloucestershire Echo* reported:

> Steve Brain, who won his ninth cheese said; 'The adrenalin rush when you get to the bottom is brilliant!' Jonathan Smith, winning his first cheese said, 'I don't know how I managed to keep on my feet but it was a fantastic feeling.' Claire Carter, winner of the women's race that year said, 'My mother, brother and cousin have all won, so I guess we are all a bit brainless.'

The same year, the County Air Ambulance had to be called not as a result of injury to a competitor, but for two people hurt on their way home from the event. A lady injured her hip falling at a stile and a young girl fell in the crush of people moving away from the hill. She was not detained in hospital.

1997

St John's Ambulance county staff officer Tony Clarke said:

> Cheese rolling is extremely dangerous but it is a tradition. St John's Ambulance has been coming here for 50 years and we have not had a single fatality. Nobody seems to come down the hill without the benefit of alcohol. We had lots of nose-bleeds and damaged wrists and one or two head injuries.

Tony Clarke criticised the behaviour of some drunken spectators, especially those who assaulted an ambulance man:

> It is one of the more dangerous parts of this job, that we are assaulted by drunks.

Steve Brain who, in 1997 won two cheeses (but had one stolen) said that running down the hill gave him a buzz:

> You just run as fast as you can and when you fall over, you get back up quick!

And Abroad

The Americans

Extract from the *Chicago Tribune* (Associated Press) 30 May 1995:

Peril of Cheese Rolling: 18 hurt
CHELTENHAM, England – Add Cheese Rolling to your list of dangerous sports, like hang-gliding and sky-diving.

In the annual Cheese Rolling contest Monday in Cheltenham, 18 of the 20 contestants were injured, four seriously enough to be sent to the hospital.

The annual competition, in which contenders vie for a giant round cheese by rolling smaller versions down Cooper's Hill, left four contestants with broken arms and legs. Fourteen others were treated for sprains. And one spectator fell and hit her head as she tried to get a better view.

Cheese rolling on Cooper's Hill is thought to date back to pre-Roman times, when it was a fertility rite heralding the return of spring.

Article from *The Wall Street Journal* of Wednesday 2 June 1999:

Gentlemen, Start Your Cheeses – Historic Race Returns to England by Christopher Knight. Dow Jones
COOPER'S HILL, England – Tony Pither remembers fondly the good old days when life had fewer restrictions and it was OK if someone wanted to risk breaking a leg or snapping a shoulder chasing cheese down a steep hill.

'Nobody ever worried about the danger in the old days. Everybody enjoyed the atmosphere', said Mr Pither, 64 years old, who was installing safety fencing here in western England on Sunday to prepare for the controversial cheese races.

Mr Pither, chairman of the Cooper's Hill Cheese Rolling Committee, joined more than 2000 others Monday who came from across Britain to help, watch or participate in the quirky yearly races that organisers say are hundreds of years old.

As reported in the 'Wall Street Journal' in March, the races were cancelled in 1998 over fears that the steep hill and the fast-rolling cheese had become too dangerous. The event returned this year after organisers added safety measures such as more fencing and hired a mountain-rescue team to retrieve the injured from the top of the 660-foot slope. They also moved the race to noon from 6p.m. to prevent runners from drinking too long at the pub beforehand.

Monday's event went off quite decorously. The wheels of cheese behaved themselves this time, a light rain left the hill's terrain in an ideal, soft condition and only a few runners were injured. But it could have been a lot worse, Mr Pither says.

'The biggest trouble we've got with safety is the cheese – it's a missile,' he said while standing atop the hill before the races. 'We can't guarantee anybody's safety here. We put up signs and boundary fencing, but you can't stop the cheese, not completely.'

The cheese is a locally made Double Gloucester, about 12 inches in diameter and 3 to 4 inches thick, weighing 7 to 8 pounds.

Ten to 15 runners lined the top of the hill Monday for each of the four races, waiting for the wheels of cheese to be released right in front of them. The first person to touch the cheese won and got to keep it.

Participants ran, jumped and tumbled head over heels after the cheese, which out-paced them all, rolling at 30 to 40 miles an hour. Only one runner, who injured a shoulder, had to be carried off on a stretcher.

Organisers said this year's success should ensure may more years of cheese rolling.

'I don't see any reason why we should stop this,' says Robert Seex, 47, a dairy farmer who was the event's master of ceremonies Monday. 'It's a good old English tradition, and it gives something for the hooligans to do.'

The Canadians

On 8 June 1999 the *International Express* carried the following report:

'Who said a cheese roll was boring?' Bumps and bruises as ancient tradition returns. Heads got bumped, bodies got bruised and bones were all but broken. You didn't have to be crackers to take part in the cheese brigade, but you certainly had to enjoy the whiff of danger. The ancient West Country tradition that drives hoards of otherwise perfectly sane individuals to chase a 9lb Double Gloucester down the steepest slope in the county ended up with the usual crop of casualties.

One was taken to hospital with head injuries and Cheltenham computer programmer Sean Keaney, 26, dislocated his shoulder for the second time in three years.

'It's exactly the same injury again, but it won't put me off,' said Sean. 'The first bit is the worst – it looks like you're jumping off a cliff. But after that you don't think about it, it's just thump, thump, thump all the way down.'

All that 'thumping' led to the event being banned last year amid fears the race down the almost vertical Cooper's Hill in the Cotswolds, had become too perilous for competitors and spectators alike.

Renegade rollers, however, refused to be cowed, and a party of die-hards last year sent a solitary cheese down the slope at dawn, to indicate their determination to return.

Their commitment was vindicated as the event proved as popular as it has since its inception in Saxon times. The outright winner – the Big Cheese, if you will was Steve Brain, 27, who was immediately dubbed 'Treble Gloucester' after an unprecedented hat-trick of victories in the men's races.

His prize was three cheeses, which he promptly gave away. 'I really enjoy the race but I always give my cheeses away because I can't stand the taste,' he said.

In the women's section, Helen Thorpe finished first ahead of Sabrina Rimmer.

The recent injury toll led to several safety measures. Races began at midday instead of 6pm to ensure competitors were sober, and safety nets prevented 40mph cheeses hitting onlookers.

Derbyshire's Mountain Rescue Team provided cover at the top of the hill while St John's Ambulance picked up the pieces at the bottom.

Organiser Tony Peasley said: 'We were all disappointed last year but we had to cancel for safety reasons. Personally I don't know why they do it – I think they must see it as a challenge.'

The South Africans

In the *South African* free ads newspaper:

Madcap Cheese rollers Stick to 'Risky' Sport.

Cooper's Hill, (England). Cheese rolling is a potentially dangerous activity. You are warned that you are present entirely at your own risk,' signs by the local municipal authority warned sternly.

But the cheering spectators who made the trek to a remote hillside in south-west England brushed aside fears as the cheese hurtled down the steep slope pursued by a dozen men. Seconds later, crumpled bodies lay writhing on the ground, surrounded by teams of green-attired paramedics.

The madcap residents of the tiny Gloucestershire village of Brockworth risked life and limb this week to preserve an ancient tradition spanning centuries; an annual Cheese Rolling competition. The bizarre contest, in which competitors dash down a 45-degree slope chasing a 3.6 kilogram Double Gloucester cheese is part of a hallowed calendar of time-honoured eccentricities in Britain.

The Japanese

The following article was published in *The Japan Times* and *The Student Japan Times* on Friday 23 July 1999. It was written in English but also contains Japanese subtitles with numbered references. I am grateful to the editor for sending me a clear copy to enable me to scan the Japanese characters.

■**イギリスのチーズ転がし大会**
（見出し）(is) ripe for ～ ～の準備が整っている（ripe には「[チーズが]熟成する」という意味もある）。
[1] Picture ～ ～を想像してみよう。typically 典型的な。glorious view すばらしい眺め。rolling green 緑の大地がなだらかに起伏する。peering down 下をのぞき見て。terrifyingly steep slope 怖いほど険しい斜面。
[3] hurl themselves 猛進する。risking 危険を冒しながら。injury けが。lose their footing 足を踏み外す。tumble head over heels まっ逆さまに転がる。(in) vain attempts to ～ ～しようとする無駄な試みで。bouncing into ～ ～に飛び込む。
[4] figment of the imagination 空想の産物。bizarre 奇想天外な。dreamed up by ～ ～が思いついた。wacky 突飛な。competition 競技大会。Gloucester 英国グロスターシャーの州都グロスター（グロスターチーズで有名）。
[5] chase ～ down ≈ ～を追いかけて≈を下る。has been ... time 時がたつうちに忘れられた。

---

[6] stepped in 介入した。spectators 観客。casualties 負傷者数。this time around 今大会。could be ... hand 片手の指で数えられた（5人以下ということ）。
[7] were brought forward 早められた。was installed 設置された。bemused 困惑した。bruises あざ。inevitable 避けられない。throw themselves ... cliff 人によってはほとんど崖と呼ぶような傾斜に身を投げ出す。
[8] was knocked unconscious 打ちつけられ意識を失った。landed on ～ ～の上に倒れた。builder 建設労働者。
[9] managed to ... feet なんとか転ばずにすませた。hurtled down 猛スピードで走り下りた。in quick succession たて続けに。
[10] entrants 参加者。applause 拍手。
[11] brave 勇敢な。charge down ～ ～に突進する。crawls はう。on hands and knees 四つんばいになって。【写真】(左端) coveted みんなが狙っていた。(中央上) pell-mell てんやわんやの。(中央下) Master of ceremonies 司会進行役。proceedings 進行。intently 一心に。

Photograph from *The Japan Times.*

Translation:

English Countryside ripe for Cheese Rolling.

Picture the scene; you're standing at the top of a hill overlooking a typically glorious view of the rolling green English countryside and peering down a terrifyingly steep slope. A man dressed in a white coat with a red flower in his breast pocket and a black top hat decorated with ribbon and holding an 8lb (3.6kg) round of cheese. After a signal from the bottom the cheese is rolled down the hill. And a group of young, and not so young men hurl themselves after it, risking serious injury as they often lose their footing and tumble head over heels in usually vain attempts to catch the cheese before bouncing into a safety net at the bottom.

This is not a figment of the imagination or a bizarre challenge dreamed up by the producers of a wacky television show, this is the Cooper's Hill Cheese Rolling competition, which for centuries has been held in the tiny village of Brockworth near the city of Gloucester.

The reason why people should want to chase cheese down a hill has been lost in the mists of time but after a break of a year for safety reasons the event made a successful return in May.

The police stepped in twelve months ago causing the historic races to be cancelled. Some thirty-three people — spectators as well as competitors — were hurt in 1996 and twenty-seven in 1997. However the casualties this time round could be counted on the fingers of one hand partly because heavy rain had made ground conditions very soft.

The times of the races were brought forward taking away drinking time in local pubs, while ski-hill type fencing was installed down the sides of the slope providing bemused watchers with extra protection from flying cheese rounds and chasers. Very little more though can be done to prevent the bruises and broken bones that are almost inevitable when people throw themselves down what some would almost view as a cliff.

Several men were hurt including one who was knocked unconscious when another competitor landed on him. However Steve Brain, a local builder, showed everyone how to do it. The amateur rugby player somehow managed to stay on his feet as he hurtled down the hill three times in quick succession to win all three men's races and three cheeses.

Helen Thorpe and Sabrina Rimmer, the only entrants in the women's race, followed the example of the cheese and rolled down the hill and over the line to great applause from some 2,000 spectators.

For those not brave enough to charge down the slope there were three races (or crawls) on hands and knees up the slope including two for children. The success of this year's races means the future of the event is safe. Brain, who has now won thirteen of the specially made cheeses says he will be back again next May, although he added, 'I don't think the cheese really matters – to be honest, I don't even like it!

The French

On 13 August 2000 the following article appeared in the colour supplement of *Le Progrès*, a daily newspaper produced in Lyon, France:

> *Tandis que le mois de mai fait chanter les oiseaux et fleurir les pâquerettes, des hordes de jeunes et moins jeunes gens aux mollets musclés se dirigent vers Cooper Hill, une colline haute de 287m, non loin de Gloucester.*
>
> *A 14 heures exactement, débute le Cooper's Hill Cheese Roll, ce qui pourrait se traduire par: « A la poursuite du fromage roulant », une tradition veille de deux cents ans.*
>
> *Le fromage en question est un Double Gloucester, fabriqué par la fromagère locale, Diana Smart, une roue de presque 30cm de diamètre, qui pèse 4kg; il reviendra à celui qui l'attrapera. Le Double Gloucester, posé sur la tranche, démarre; une foule se lance à sa poursuite. Mais comme la pente est effroyablement raide – de 60° en haute à 40° en bas – , peu nombreux sont ceux qui parviennent à rester debout. Le public observe un fromage guilleret qui atteint les 50km/h, suivi d'un magma de bras, de jambes et de rires.*
>
> *Certaines années, on a relevé jusqu'à 24 concurrents, 7 spectaeurs et 2 ambulanciers diversement abimés. Un homme a voulu éviter un gloucester fou, a trébuché et s'est retrouvé 287m plus bas.*
>
> *En 1997, le gagnant, Craig Carter, s'est cassé le bras gauche; pendant que les infirmiers le soignaient, un être sans moralité lui a fauché le fromage.*

Translated:

> As during the month of May the birds sing and the daisies flower, hoards of young and not so young people with flabby muscles make their way towards Cooper's Hill, a hill that is 287m high, not far from Gloucester.
>
> At exactly 2 o'clock, Cooper's Hill Cheese Roll begins, an event which may be described as 'The chase of the round cheese', a tradition that is 200 years old.
>
> The cheese in question is a Double Gloucester, made by a local cheese-maker, Diana Smart, a wheel of about 30cm. diameter, which weighs 4kg: it will go to whoever catches it. The Double Gloucester, perched on the edge starts off; a crowd launch themselves in pursuit. But as the slope is horrifyingly steep – 60 degrees at the top 40 degrees at the bottom – only a few are left standing. The public watch a cheese happily reaching 50km/h, followed by a jumble of arms, legs and laughter.

Cartoon from French daily newspaper *Le Progress.*

Some years one can count up to 24 contestants, 7 spectators and 2 ambulance-men with various degrees of injury. One man avoided a mad Double Gloucester, stumbled and found himself 287m lower down.

In 1997, the winner, Craig Carter, broke his left arm; while the nurses treated him, someone stole the cheese.

[A slightly inaccurate, but rather amusing account as seen by a French reporter!]

five

The Cheese

The *Victoria County History* records the Barton Street Fair in Gloucester. In 1586 it was described as a pig fair, but later became widely known as a cheese fair serving the rich dairying region of the Vale of Gloucester. The volume of cheese brought to the fair declined towards the end of the eighteenth century as the practice of buying it directly from the farms became more common. The fair still attracted enough of that commodity, however, for it to be described as 'our great cheese fair' in 1792. It also became the city's principal pleasure fair attracting peddlers, gypsies and travelling showmen. Barton Street is a continuation of Painswick Road which leads directly through the village of Upton-St-Leonards to Cooper's Hill. Could there be a connection between the cheese fair and the Cooper's Hill Cheese Rolling ceremony? There is certainly a 'cheesy' environment. It is not certain when real cheese was first used for the Cheese Rolling ceremony. The Gloucester Folk Museum holds what were thought to be three substitute wooden 'cheeses' used during the Second World War.

So, when were these old wooden 'cheeses' used? Were they the forerunners of real cheese? Were they 'cheeses' at all? Further investigation at the Folk Museum produced some more information.

Cheese 1

Bound with iron, this cheese has a diameter of about seven inches. It was part of a collection of articles owned by Dr Oliver Wild. He was a well-known collector of old and unusual items and presented this to the museum sometime in the 1930s. It was obviously old at that time as it is very battered and worn. On 26 November 1998, this cheese was one of the items shown on the BBC antiques quiz programme *Going for a Song* where it was described as a wooden cheese used at Cooper's Hill in wartime. The expert suggested that it had been made in 1920 and he valued it at £60.

Cheese 2

This cheese formed part of a collection. It belonged to Maj. H.J. Lloyd-Johns who lived in Witcombe, a village at the foot of Cooper's Hill. It is made of *lignum vitae*, a very dense hardwood. The museum acquired this one in about 1942 but it was extremely old even at the time that it was donated.

Cheese 3

Given to the museum in 1972 by a lady living in Newnham, Gloucestershire, this cheese is also made of *lignum vitae* and is quite battered. It is described as, 'possibly a wooden cheese used at Cooper's Hill'. Could it actually have been used in another sport? According to the museum curator items were sometimes used for more than one purpose. Might it be an old wood used in bowls, or some similar game? Could it have been part of a cheese press? Shall we ever know? We are certain, however, that none of these three 'cheeses' were used as recently as the Second World War.

A wartime wooden substitute was used from 1941-1954 when food rationing was imposed. That cheese, however, is held privately by a resident of Cooper's Hill and in appearance is very like a real cheese. It was wrapped in white paper and decorated with red and blue ribbons just as the present-day real cheese. It has, under the wrapping, a small hollow which contained a very small token piece of real cheese so that the tradition of rolling real cheese could continue. It is certain that this cheese was the only one used at the time because winners of the races had to walk back up the hill with the cheese for it to be used in the following race!

The wooden 'cheese' that was used from 1941-1954 (Jean Jefferies)

Cheese 1, iron-bound 'cheese', part of a collection owned by Dr Oliver Wild. (Jean Jefferies)

Cheese 2, part of a collection of Maj. H.J. Lloyd-Johns. (Jean Jefferies)

Cheese 3, made of *lignum vitae*. (Jean Jefferies)

On 14 May 1937 this advertisement appeared in *The Citizen* newspaper:

GO TO
COOPER'S HILL WAKE
ON BANK HOLIDAY
AND
SEE THE CHEESE ROLLING

THESE CHEESES ARE SUPPLIED BY
CULL & CO.
25 ST ALDATE STREET

It is said that cheeses used for rolling have weighed up to 35lbs. Certainly, records show a Double Gloucester cheese used in 1938 weighed 28lbs.

In more recent years the Double Gloucester cheeses used weigh between 7lbs-8lbs. The cheeses are kept in their cheese-cloth, wrapped in polythene, with a card-board disc on each side and then tightly bound with white plastic tape to prevent disintegration as they are rolled down the 1 in 2 slope. They are decorated with a red / blue cross on each side.

> One to be ready!
> Two to be steady!
> Three to prepare!
> (the cheese is released at the word 'three')
> And Four to be off!

At this point the competitors hurl themselves down the hill after the cheese. The rolled cheese is never caught by the competitors (unless it veers off course) as it reaches estimated speeds of 70 miles per hour. Runners are usually unable to stop and are caught by 'catchers', local rugby players, at the bottom of the hill. The first person to reach the bottom of the hill wins the cheese! Competitors in 2nd. and 3rd. places receive cash prizes. The cheeses are rolled by local well-known personalities.

Occasionally a cheese has broken up on its way down the slope and there are stories of cheeses bouncing over the cottage at the bottom.

In 1910, the cheese was described as 'a disc of wood wrapped in pink paper that was exchanged at the top of the hill for a prize cheese'. Nineteen years later, in 1929, a real cheese is obviously used as an article tells how 'the cheese suffers rather badly during its career down the hill, bits fly off at angles'.

It was said that the winner of the race was the person who managed to 'capture' the largest piece of broken cheese. In 1933, a newspaper article stated

> In recent times large coloured discs have been substituted for the cheese itself in the chase downhill, for it was often found that the cheese had been badly damaged in the descent, and it was sometimes almost uneatable by the time the successful competitors secured it.

The article went on to say:

> An amusing incident happened with the chase. It was a rule that no competitor should, in his pursuit climb any hedge.
>
> The necessity for this was in fact completely eliminated since the disc representing the cheese, though it bounded over a hedge into a garden, bounced over the opposite hedge into the roadway, where it was finally captured.

In 1941, because of wartime restrictions and rationing, a wooden replica cheese was substituted for real cheese. It had a concealed hole that held a tiny piece of real cheese, thus maintaining the tradition of rolling real cheese.

In 1945 an article in *The Citizen* of 23 May about food rationing mentioned that the individual ration of cheese was 2oz per week.

The minutes of the Cheese Rolling Committee in 1954 decided that: 'As cheese was now de-rationed, efforts should be made to obtain at least one real cheese.'

In that year however, only one real cheese was rolled and that was for the first race. It is reported that it broke up on its descent. The wooden 'dummy' cheese was used for the other three races. The fourteen-year-old ladies' winner was presented with a 5lb Dutch cheese as a prize and the two other winners went home with 10s each. Since then real cheeses have been rolled and the wooden 'dummy' assigned to the cupboard and history. Cheeses have been supplied and in many cases kindly donated by several different cheese makers:

1955	Four cheeses were given by Messrs J. Walter Thompson.
1956	Messrs Vickers were suppliers.
1957	The supplier is unknown, but they were reported to be 7lb Caerphilly cheeses.
1958	The cheeses were presented by the Cheese Bureau and were New Zealand Cheddar.
1959	Messrs Thurston of Newent.
1960	Mr R.N. Look of Ditcheat, Shepton Mallet offered one Double Gloucester cheese. Three more and a spare were purchased from Calvers, a Brockworth shop.
1961-1973	The cheeses were presented by the maker of the cheese, Mr Look.

Mrs Margaret Brentnall produced an article in 1965 quoting:

> The cheeses were produced on the farm of Mr R.N. Look, near Ditcheat, Shepton Mallet, Somerset. The Double Gloucester is a mellow 'hard-pressed' cheese. It has a smooth texture and is similar to Cheddar but slightly pinker. The cheeses made for the races measured ten inches in diameter, two inches in depth and weighed about 9lbs. They were protected by a wooden casing so that they were still in excellent condition at the end of the race'.

1974 and 1975	Mrs Martell of Dymock made the cheese. (In 2005 Martells shot to fame as the makers of Stinking Bishop featured in the film *Wallace and Grommet and the Were Rabbit*.)
1976-1983	Castle Carey Dairies of Somerset.
1984-1987	Mr John Crisp of Newent. Beverley Belben wrote in *The Citizen*, 1984:

> John Crisp and his wife Dorothy made cheese from the milk of their own Gloucester cattle and Ayrshire milk bought in. They made traditional double Gloucester, using the same method used in the county in the 1600s, as well as single Gloucester. It takes about 1 gallon of milk to produce 1lb of cheese. Each cheese is pressed for two days under a weight of about 1 ton. It is then stored as it matures for four months.

Cheese Today

Mrs Diana Smart of Old Ley Court, Churcham, makes Single Gloucester and Haresfield (a Parmesan-style hard cheese) as well as Double Gloucester cheeses. She has been the supplier of the Double Gloucester cheeses that are used for the Cheese Rolling since 1988. The cheese made by Mrs Smart is handmade using whole milk from a mixed herd of Brown Swiss, Holstein and Gloucester cows. She is the only person in Gloucestershire who now makes Double Gloucester cheese by hand using traditional methods. The process takes a day from pumping about 100galls of milk from the morning milking into a vat, heating to 19°-20°C, and adding a starter (a bacterial culture that works on the lactose in the milk and turning it into lactic acid) to pressing the cheeses in the moulds, or truckles.

On the following pages are Mrs Smart, at her farm, working throughout the day, making Double Gloucester cheese. Curds are formed during the morning after the starter has been added and the resulting whey has been drained off. The curds are cut to make channels for more drainage.

(All cheese-making photographs, Jean Jefferies)

Right: The curds are cut to make channels for more drainage.

Below: Curds are cut and doubled-up.

Left: Draining whey from the vat.

Below: Squeezing more whey from the curds.

Right: Strips of solid curd milked to break up the curds into manageable pieces to put into the moulds.

Below: Fine sea-salt is added to the milled curds as more strips are put through the mill.

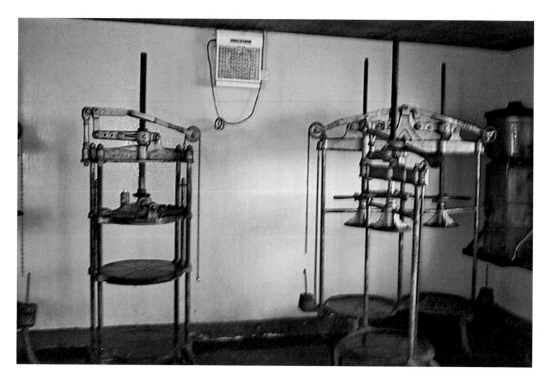

Cheese presses.

Mrs Smart weighing cheese at the point of sale.

Above and right: The pressed cheeses are kept in the cold-store for several months. As they mature they produce a spectacular fungus which helps to ripen the cheese, form the rind and produce its final flavour. The fungus is washed off before the cheeses are sold.

Opposite page: The final product, a fine Double Gloucester cheese. (Jean Jefferies)

Below: A winning cheese in the hands of a champion. (Jean Jefferies)

six

The Maypole

The maypole surmounted by a cockerel, marks the top of the slope that is the site of the annual Cooper's Hill Cheese Rolling ceremony. It is said that the pole was once a true maypole, danced around by girls for a ribbon prize. As the hill eroded through the years the site of the maypole became closer to the cliff edge and dancing around it was no longer possible. Traditionally, the maypole came from the woods on the Witcombe Estate. At one time it seems it was replaced annually. The tree was dragged to the summit by a horse and erected by local people, using ropes, but later the process was mechanised and a tractor was used. In years gone by a bunch of gorse was attached to the middle of the maypole in the belief that it would drive away the devil as well as ensure a good harvest. In 1908 *The Gloucester Journal* reported that a new pole was presented by Mr Dyer Edwards. There is a reference in 1931 to villagers digging up and re-erecting the maypole on Whit Sunday evening. The pictures on the following pages show the various stages of the erecting of the maypole through the years and it is interesting to see how the methods used in hoisting it have progressed through time, during which manpower and horse power have eventually given way to mechanical means. A tractor was first used in 1965.

In 1945 the weathercock blew off its pole due to severe weather and had to be replaced.

In 1948 the pole blew down in a gale and a new one was donated by Mr Hicks-Beach of Witcombe Estate. Photographs taken at the time show the gorse being attached halfway up the pole.

On 9 March 1999 the maypole was found on the ground. It seemed to have been pushed over – there was no sign of rot at the point of severance and the weathercock had disappeared. The cockerel was found several months later nailed to a fence. The broken stunted pole was later put back after the 1999 Cheese Rolling and Wake but it was not replaced with a new one. This is possibly the only year that the Cheese Rolling and Wake ever took place without the maypole.

Left: The maypole.

Below: An old photograph which appeared in *The Citizen* newspaper, 1924.

Opposite above: 1948. From left to right: Ted Bradbeer, Roy Mitchell, Bill Gregory, Bill Jones, -?-, Bert Mitchell, Len Millard, -?-, Jim Hall. Sitting on the pole: Ted Millard (fixing the gorse) and Tom Windo (with dog). (Roy Mitchell)

Opposite below: Len Millard and Bert Mitchell fix the cockerel to the top of the maypole, 1956. (Roy Mitchell)

Above and left: Bert Mitchell with the cockerel in 1965. (Roy Mitchell)

Opposite above: Ted Millard and Bert Mitchell attach the gorse. (Roy Mitchell)

Opposite below: Ready to lift, 1965. (Roy Mitchell)

Left: In 1965 Mr A.W. Davis gave a new pole and the cockerel was repaired after the pole was sawn down by a group of people calling themselves the Society for Cutting Down Old Trees. (*The Citizen*)

Below: Replacing the pole in 1965. From left to right: Peter Astman, James Searight. Behind: Brian Millard, ?William Davis, Bert Mitchell. Right of pole: Ted Hall, –?–, Don Brommage, Len Millard, –?–, Bill Cooper, Arthur Bick (MC at the time). In the hole: Bill Jones. (*The Citizen*)

The next seven pictures: Replacing the maypole, 23 February 1983. (Joy Macdonald)

Replacing the maypole, 23 February 1983. (Joy Macdonald)

seven

Children's Sports and 'Scrambling for Buns'

A newspaper report in *The Gloucester Journal* of 13 June 1908 describes the Cheese Rolling and Wake and mentions numerous attractions that included a programme of 'children's sports' and 'scrambling for buns'.

Sadly the numerous attractions no longer take place and there are no children's sports. However, scrambling for sweets does take place. When all the Cheese Rolling races have finished, handfuls of sweets are thrown from the top of the hill and children scramble for them. Was this custom symbolic of scattering seeds? It has been suggested that it might be a survival of some fertility rite, performed in the hope of producing a good harvest. It must be remembered that in earlier years the Cheese Rolling and Wake was held at midsummer, a time much closer to harvest time than our present-day spring bank holiday.

The development of this part of the Wake is difficult to plot. Because the Cheese Rolling itself is such a dramatic event, few reports have been made through the years about the other attractions. In 1908 the programme mentioned 'children's sports and scrambling for buns'. A newspaper report of events in 1941 includes the information that 'novelty events included a scramble for sweets'. Minutes of committee meetings from 1942 give some idea of modern developments. Sweets were of course rationed during the war. In 1942 sweets were used but in 1943, 1944 and 1945 potato crisps were scattered on the hill instead. Sweets were obtainable, but the wartime ration was only 2oz per person per week (roughly equivalent to eight small squares of chocolate) so not readily available for scattering around. In 1946, 'Mr Jones was asked to see if he could manage to find some sweets' instead of crisps (*The Citizen*).

One edition of *The Citizen* confirms that sweets were scattered that year. In 1957 a decision was made to reintroduce biscuits as well as sweets (7lb biscuits and 10lbs sweets) but no other mention of biscuits has been found. (The 10lb of sweets used in 1957 was more than the ration for one person per year in wartime! At 2oz per week, a year's ration was only about 6lb). From 1947 to the present day sweets have been provided for this part of the Wake. On many occasions they have been kindly donated by local residents.

Tom Windo (MC 1934–1955) scattering fruit cake in the 1930s. (Eric Tomkins)

Tug-of-War and Children's Races

Details of the tug-of-war through the years are fairly sketchy with most of the information coming from the minutes of the committee as event plans rather than retrospective reports. The events themselves may well have been altered on the day. Results of the contests were not often recorded. In 1910 the tug-of-war between ladies and gentlemen was captained by Miss Ethel Priday and Revd J.H. Seabrook.

1941–1942

Committee minutes give details of plans for a tug-of-war and sports on the hill near the maypole. There were to be flat races for boys and girls and prize money would be: first 1s 6d; second 1s; third 6d.

1943–1944

There would be a tug-of-war for fifteen ladies and fifteen gents, also one for Army versus Air Force as well as the children's flat races.

1946

The tug-of-war was for men versus women.

1947

The Citizen reported that German POWs won the tug-of-war.

1949

The Citizen in its annual report said, 'a tug-of-war was held at the top of the hill in an interval.'

1950

In 1950 Brockworth Scouts constructed an aerial runway, which proved to be very popular throughout the evening. Children's races and a tug-of-war seem to have formed the regular pattern of events.

1951

After considerable interference from the crowd the previous year, the tug-of-war did not take place.

1952

The tug-of-war was reintroduced for married versus single men and married versus single women.

A winner of a children's race in the 1930s, with Tom Windo MC and Mrs Buckle. (Eric Tomkins)

1956

Two teams of Young Farmers competed with teams from Gloucester and Stroud.

1957

Two teams of scouts competed.

1960

Prize money for the tug-of war teams was to be £2 for the winners and £1 for the losers – presumably for the team to share! Mention is made again of the children's races. In view of the numbers of competitors the races were to be restricted to children aged six to eleven years.

1961

The tug-of war was between the British Legion and Brockworth Youth Club.

1962

A report of the annual event in *The Citizen* tells of the entertainment provided by the Gloucestershire Morris Dancers under the leadership of Mr Ron Upton.

1971

The tug-of-war was between eight men versus fourteen ladies and children's race prizes were decimalised to 10p, 5p and 3p.

1973

Race winners only, received a prize of 20p.

1976

From this date children up to ten years only were allowed to race.

1978–1981

There was to be a junior tug-of war for children up to the age of twelve and a senior tug-of-war for eight stewards versus twelve ladies.

1982

It was decided that stewards could not take part because of crowd trouble during the previous year. Instead the contest was to be Hucclecote Old Boys Club versus Brockworth Rugby Club. Prizes for the children's races were increased to 20p, 10p and 5p.

1984

In view of lack of support, there were no children's flat running races. Instead, an uphill race was introduced for children up to twelve. Junior and senior tug-of-war contests were retained.

1985

It seems that some difficulties were experienced with the senior tug-of-war this year.

1986

The senior tug-of-war was abandoned although the junior event continued until 1994 after which there is no further mention of it in the committee minutes.

2005

There were no longer any events taking place at the top of the hill. There were two uphill races, one for boys under twelve years and one for girls. The winners received a small Double Gloucester cheese.

eight

Myths, Legends and Art

Mystery surrounds the origins of the Cooper's Hill Cheese Rolling and Wake. It is unlikely that the real facts will ever be known. Local people have their own ideas and beliefs about it all and there are some fictional stories that have been told. Other people have interpreted their ideas in works of art – poetry, embroidery and painting. Bert Mitchell lived on the hill with his family and he was very involved with the event for many years, being a committee member from 1946. Here are his thoughts on the subject:

A Legend of Cheese Rolling on Cooper's Hill
By Bert Mitchell (1892-1984)

Here once stood a cottage where rabbits now roam,
And a couple called Cooper they made it their home.
But that's all disappeared, oh so long ago
And all that is left is a legend or so.

Mrs Cooper was house proud, she dusted and mopped
Week in and week out, she scarce ever stopped.
So spotless her carpets, so polished each door
You could shave in a panel or dine off the floor.

Old Cooper made cheeses, but 'Oh!' said his wife
'Those cheeses are truly the bane of my life.
He leaves them on tables, he leaves them on chairs,
And this morning I found a large cheese on the stairs!'

This went on for years, till one day she swore
'I can stand it no longer this is the last straw.
Just look at this cheese on my clean window-sill!'
And she gave it a shove and it rolled down the hill.

It whizzed past his head and Old Cooper gave chase
And caught it and brought it back safe! 'What a race
That would make for the lads of the village' he mused,
'Though it's not quite the way I like cheese to be used.'

So that's how it started and today people flock
Where an alder in top hat, beribboned his smock,
Sends lads chasing down the hillside below,
Just like Mr Cooper did long, long ago.

Another account, fictitious yet woven around facts and possibilities, was written by Col. Thomson. He was also a resident of the hill, and a committee member until his death, thought to be in 1941-42. His story, written under the name 'Miles', appeared in *The Gloucester Journal* on 23 May 1914:

The Bel Fires

The lights of Gloucester to the west, and Cheltenham to the east were just beginning to twinkle vaguely as David Montgomery stood on the top of Cooper's hill on the 16th. June, watching a number of young men lowering the May pole which stands at the edge of the steep slope looking northwards to 'Chosen' Hill.

He strolled up to the workers while they were resting for a moment before the pole was finally allowed to fall, and asked an elderly man what they were doing. The patriarch explained at great length that the May pole had to be lowered once a year on the eve of Whit Sunday, or the villagers of Cooper's Hill and Brockworth would lose their Common rights of grazing and wood gleaning over all the Cooper's Hill Common.

He said that the young men of the village lowered and raised this May pole, which rivalled in size the mast of some huge 'amiral', while he, as the oldest man in the village, superintended and shared the labourers' cider.

The huge mast began to tilt, and was lowered with surprising skill by the young men, and while some of them fastened a collar of green bushes half-way up it one youth explained that the village had 'writings' of this having been done every year for 500 years. No one, however, knew why should be or had, apparently, given a thought to the origin of the custom which they had known and accepted all their lives.

Slowly the mast was raised again and secured, and the young men went off with loud yells which informed the Cooper's Hill Commoners that the yearly 'corvee' had been duly rendered.

David cautiously picked his way in the moonlight down the steep face, and sought the cottage at the foot where he was lodging, and went to bed, not, however, to sleep.

About midnight he got up, thinking he heard shouts from the May pole, and looked up the bank.

At first nothing was visible except the green hill showing white in the moonlight, and the pole with its weathercock against the horizon.

Thinking he had been dreaming, David was turning away when he again thought he heard shouts, and was nearly sure he saw some dim figures moving against the sky at the top of the

Olive Bushell is an artist living in nearby Brockworth. In the 1940s she won a painting competition with a picture that was similar to this one.

bank. The shouts turned into a kind of chaunt, making a great volume of sound, and the figures seemed to dance up and down and move round and round in a circle, and a glare of light shone out round the May pole.

Hastily jumping into some of his clothes he left his room wondering why none of the cottage dwellers had been roused by the clamour. When, however, he got outside all was still, no noise was to be heard and nothing was to be seen when he looked up at the May pole. Somewhat mystified he went back to bed and to a troubled sleep.

The next morning he was surprised to find how clearly the impression of the fleeting midnight scene had stayed with him, and being by blood pure Welsh, that is to say pure Celt, he could not help the incident praying on his mind. By the evening, however he had forgotten it, and by the morning of Whit Monday was much interested to hear of the 'show' which was to come of that afternoon at the May pole.

Hundreds of people from the surrounding villages and the more distant Gloucester came to the top of the hill to watch young men run furiously down the precipitous bank after cheeses which were rolled down from the May pole as prizes for the reckless youth who could first catch the cheese.

The boys and girls ran races, the old women told how, when they were young women they used to dance under the May pole every Whit Monday; the local squire, the local parson, and a leading Commoner superintended the sports and started the cheeses down the hill, and David Montgomery watched and looked out over the wonderful view. Gloucester to the West, with its Cathedral showing huge over the house-tops; to the East Cheltenham, and Birdlip up which the Irmin Street ran straight as an arrow; North-west the Malverns and far to the West the hills of Hereford and Brecknock.

Above: This cartoon is signed by W.J. Linton (1812-1898) who was a Victorian cartoonist, engraver and book illustrator. He lived in Hampstead, North London. It is quite possible that it may have no connection at all with the local event.

Left: This cartoon, found in a scrap-book, is entitled Chasing the Cheese. It is of unknown origin with both the signature and date unclear. It describes the Cheese Rolling taking place on Birdlip Hill, near Cooper's Hill, a common mistake for people unfamiliar with the area.

Opposite above: Cartoon (unknown origin).

Chasing the monster cheese at Birdlip.

He had never been there before, but there was a strange and uneasy feeling in his brain that the country was familiar, that even the gathering of folk and the shouts when the cheeses were rolled were familiar. However, by seven in the evening the sports were over, and the crowd had melted away, leaving Celtic David alone at the top of the bluff.

The curious feeling of familiarity still remained with him as he went down to the cottage; he could not eat or settle down, and towards ten o'clock he climbed the hill again, sat down under a tree at the edge of the cliff, and looked out over the moonlit landscape.

At this point in the story it is necessary to say a word about this dreamy young man who was groping in his inner consciousness after vague impressions of by-gone generations.

David was, as has been said, a pure-born Celt. Born and bred in Montgomeryshire, near Machynlleth, of Welsh-speaking parents, he had absorbed all the Celtic legends he could get anyone to tell him, had learnt music and played the harp at local Eisteddfods. In person he was the typical Brython Celt, with the round head, black hair, black eyes and fair skin of the Celt unmixed with any Saxon or Norse strain.

He had been ill, and having 'run down' a good deal after hard work in Bristol, had been sent by the doctor to Cooper's Hill to pick up again.

It will therefore be realised that he was in a frame of body and mind favourable to dreaming dreams and seeing visions.

For some time he sat in the warm June night listening to the subdued hoots of the owls, and the rustling of the rabbits in the brushwood. Gradually drowsiness overcame him, and he dropped on the bank fast asleep.

Suddenly he woke with a start to find that it was broad daylight. He was still on the bluff, but the May pole was not there. In its place was an altar made rudely of earth and stones, beside which stood a thick pole about six feet high, the top of which was rudely carved into the shape of a head.

He glanced round, but, though the hills and plains seemed unchanged, no cities were to be seen, no Gloucester Cathedral, no wide ribbons of roads, no villages; and the country was un-enclosed and sparsely cultivated. He looked down at his body. He was dressed in rudely-cut and roughly-dressed skins. His feet and head were bare.

Before the altar he saw two splendid-looking, elderly men dressed in white, with long beards. Scattered about were a few other men, a few of whom had woven cloth garments, but most of whom were dressed as David was. One of these came up to David and asked, in Welsh, who he was and whence he came.

David, to his surprise, found himself answering that he had come from Machynlleth, on a mission to one of the Chiefs of a tribe who live in the Buckholt Forest and that he had lost his way.

'Then,' said the man, 'you are in time for a great ceremony. The priests and the victims will be here almost at once.'

Seeing that David did not understand, he said, 'We have stormed the Roman camp on Painswick Hill over there to the East. We killed all the Romans but we captured a good many of their traitorous British auxiliaries, and these will be burnt in the "figure" tonight. First of all, however, the 'god-king' will be sacrificed on the altar here before the 'god' figure on the pole, to insure us good crops, and fortune in war, during the coming year.'

This did not surprise David in his character of Ancient Britain, for the burning of criminals and prisoners of war was carried out by his own tribe, but the sacrifice of the 'god-king' he had never seen, though he knew it was a very much older rite only resorted to when tribal misfortunes had weighed heavily on the people.

He and his friend climbed one of the small trees and looked down on the green plateau.

From every quarter crowds of men, women and children were pouring in and grouping themselves round an open spot. They were evidently restless and excited, and the priests had some difficulty in keeping a clear space round the altar.

The sun was dropping over the lower reaches of the Severn, when a sound of horns was heard, and a murmur arose from the crowd, which swelled into a shout as a procession of white-robed priests arrived escorting a magnificent young man, and four young women, who were all brought up to the altar. The young man was obviously in a state of religious exaltation, and walked proudly as if to his wedding. The women had equally obviously been drugged, and were dragged along in an almost insensible state.

A shout arose, 'It is the God with his attendants!'

David heard, all around him, shouts of welcome and anxious queries as to whether he would voluntarily immolate himself or whether he would struggle.

The High Priest approached the altar, and an elaborate ritual began in a language, which the spectators evidently did not understand. Finally the High Priest pointed to the sun, now setting crimson and gibbous over the Welsh mountains, and cried in a terrible voice, 'All is now ready for the victim!' and was answered by a roar from the swaying crowd, 'The victim! The victim!'

The young man, drawing a long breath, walked firmly up to the High Priest, and knelt. The High Priest plunged a knife into his throat, and dragging him to the altar laid him prostrate on it. Other priests seized the women to slaughter them on the edge of the cliff; a woman shrieked under the tree, a branch broke and our young Briton fell stunned and bruised into the crowd.

When he recovered his senses, he found that it was dark. The women had all run away or had been chased away, and the priests were standing on the edge of the cliff and handing out wheels made of boughs which were set alight and rolled down the steep bank.

The young men of the tribes, who all seemed frantic with religious fervour and drink, rushed recklessly down the dark slope after the blazing wheels. Here and there huge bonfires were blazing, over which the less enterprising men were leaping backward and forward, while over the altar towered two huge wicker figures shaped roughly like human beings. From these issued groans and cries, the sound of which seemed still more, if possible, to excite the crowds. David knew that inside the figures were the prisoners of war who were to be burnt alive as a sacrifice to Baal.

David heard that they were all Britons of a distant tribe who were allies of the Romans; all the Roman soldiers had died fighting, or had committed suicide rather than be taken alive.

A confused sound of horns arose. The priests called for silence and began another ritual chant with an extraordinarily high, penetrating chorus. The chorus ceased. The High Priest took a torch and set fire to one of the huge figures, while another priest lit the other. The dry basket-work crackled; an appalling yell rose from the figures, growing louder and louder as the fire took hold, only to be drowned by yells of joy from the crowd.

The moon rose higher and higher, the chorus re-commenced shriller and yet more shrill when suddenly a loud and piercing trumpet note was heard. It was answered by other trumpet peals from all four sides. Two or three soldiers with gleaming breast-plates showed amongst the trees. The trumpets sounded again. A tall man carrying a brass eagle on top of a staff stepped into the open; swiftly behind him deployed the legionaries.

The Roman General, Agricola, the legate of Caesar, whose head-quarters were at Cirencester, had taken his steps well on learning of this assembly; and a short march from the Irmyn Street had sufficed to surround the un-suspecting crowd.

A third quite different trumpet call was heard. 'The kites know well the long stern swell, that bids the Romans close.'

The terrified and undisciplined multitude made a dash down the shadowy slopes of the hill, only to run against the weapons of another body of soldiers: not legionaries these, but allies whose brethren had been immolated.

Back they surged and tried to form round the altar and the High Priest. Closer and closer pressed the iron line of soldiers. Deeper and deeper hewed the Roman sword into the desperate, surging crowd, whilst above all the two wicker figures blazed.

The High Priest climbed on to the altar just as the two figures collapsed with a crash; with a loud call on the God he hurled himself into the flaming pile, followed one by one, by ten other priests.

David saw a centurion, on whose horse-tail helmet the moon glittered, leap on to the altar.

He turned to fly, when a soldier struck him on the head with his sword, and – he awoke to find the moon sinking over the plain and the dawn breaking over Cheltenham, allowing the first gleams of the rising sun to strike on the tower of Gloucester Cathedral in the distance.

The Cheese Rolling was even featured in an advertisement (date and origin unknown).

Transcript of the above advertisement:

HISTORY OF CHEESE No 14

AN OLD CHEESE CUSTOM

At Cooper's Hill, near Gloucester, every Whitsun, cheeses are rolled down the steep slope by the leading people of the neighborhood, and the inhabitants chase the cheeses down the hill.

The starter is dressed in a white chemise and gaily beribboned top-hat. Our picture shows this ancient custom in Shakespeare's day.

The custom celebrates the granting of dairy-farming rights.

Celebrate these rights by eating Chedlet Cheese on all occasions Refined cheddar flavour.

CHEDLET CHEESE

Write for booklet, 'West Countrie Tours,' with road maps (FREE). Dept. J., Aplin & Barrett & the Western Counties Creameries Ltd., Yeovil, Somerset

The following poem was published in summer 1998. It followed the cancellation of the public Wake of that year:

Cooper's Hill Cheese Roll by Nilda Sharpe (pseudonym)

For centuries, or so it's told,
Down Cooper's Hill a cheese was rolled.
And on Whit Mondays it took place
In each and every year of grace.

But in this year of ninety-eight
The County Council men did state
(Just to prove that they've no soul)
'Down Cooper's Hill no cheese shall roll!'
But we are men of Gloucestershire,
No Council's going to quench our fire,
Nor break with our tradition.
The cheese was rolled – we saw it go!
And we'll proclaim it – even though
We're sentenced for sedition.

How it all began! by Maureen Pither

Now there was once a dragon on Cooper's Hill,
I wonder if he lives there still?
He was not so big, so I've been told,
And he wasn't brave, and he wasn't bold.
In fact most folk did not know he was there
(if they heard his snoring they did not care).
Imagine the shock when one fine day
He went berserk in a really big way
Such a roaring never before was heard
And he stamped his feet so very hard,
That the rocks and boulders tumbled down
Onto the people of Brockworth town.
No-one wanted to face this foe,
Except one boy who decided to go
And see this dragon upon the hill –
No longer sleepy, no longer still.
Up he climbed, to his mother's dismay.
They watched ALL day, and they waited ALL night,
Then back he came as the sun brought daylight,
Had he seen the dragon? Was there a fight?
'No', said the boy, 'it was quite alright'.
He'd helped the poor beast pull out a bad tooth,
And now, poor thing, it slept soundly forsooth.

So every year on a Monday evening in May,
The people celebrate that very big day
By rolling cheeses instead of boulders and stone,
To remember the boy who went all alone
To fight the dragon on Cooper's Hill –
I wonder if he lives there still?

Is this why the church at Brockworth is dedicated to St George?

Each member of Institute of the Gloucestershire Federation of Womens' Institutes was asked to work a panel depicting their particular institute to form part of a large patchwork wall hanging for display at WI House in Gloucester.

Above: Maureen Pither who wrote the poem on page 107 also made this beautiful collage illustrating the Cheese Roll which was the contribution from Cooper's Hill WI.

Left: Another piece of Maureen Pither's work was the entry of Cooper's Hill WI for an exhibition at Cirencester in 1969.

nine

'Rollers'

Each year, guests are invited by the Cheese Rolling Committee to roll the cheeses for the races. These 'rollers' are often committee members, local residents, local personalities, school headteachers, Church ministers, parish councillors and so on. Names of past rollers have been taken from the minutes of committee meetings. These may be inaccurate as those people who have been invited are not always able to accept their invitations. There is no record in the past of any substitutions that may have been made.

1908

Mr Priday
Revd J.H. Seabrook

1909

No record

1910 and 1911

Mr H.Y. Jones

1914

Revd J.H. Seabrook

W. (Bill) Fitzgerald Jones, 1938–1940. (Eric Tomkins)

Revd J.W. Kent, rolling in 1940. (Roy Mitchell)

1912, 1913, 1915 to 1920s

Records have not been found

1920s

Unsure of precise date, Mr William Priday of Brockworth Court Farm

1929

Mrs Buckle
Miss Ethel Priday
Col. C. Davis

1930–1937

Records have not been found

1938

Mr Robert Perkins
Miss Ethel Priday
Mr W. Fitzgerald Jones
Mr L.T. Millard

1939

Mr Robert Perkins, MP for Stroud (a 28lb cheese)
Col. W.D. Thomson
Miss Ethel Priday
Mr W. Fitzgerald Jones
Mr C. Stephens
Mr L.T. Millard

1940

Pilot Officer Robert Perkins sent a 28lb Double Gloucester cheese for the second year in succession. The cheese used was huge compared with the 7-8lb cheeses used today.

1941–1954

To continue the tradition of rolling a cheese during a time of food rationing, a wooden substitute cheese was used (see Chapter Five). There was, however, only one wooden cheese so the winner of each race had to carry it up the hill for the next race!

1941

Pilot Officer Robert Perkins, MP for Stroud, was the only roller recorded.

1942

The committee received a letter from Pilot Officer Robert Perkins asking if he could roll two wooden cheeses. It was decided to accept his offer and ask him for the prize money of 15s for the races. Cash prizes were given at this time – first 7s 6d; second 5s; third 2s 6d. Other rollers were:

Miss Ethel Priday
Mr Stephens
Capt. John Davis

Minutes of the Cheese Rolling Committee have been available from 1942. At this point Miss Ethel Priday was chairman (and until her death in 1947) and had possibly held this post for several years previously. It seems that people who rolled the cheeses were usually committee members which explains their frequent appearance in the list. One cheese was to be rolled for ladies only, one for boys only and one for the members of the Forces only. Two would be open for anyone to chase.

1943

It was agreed to send five wooden cheeses down the hill. Rollers were:
Flt Lt Robert Perkins
Maj. C. Taylor (from Eastbourne)
Miss Ethel Priday (chairman of the committee)
Mr W. Jones
Mr L. Millard

Right: Mrs Buckle. (Eric Tomkins)

Far right: Len Millard has just rolled a cheese. (Eric Tomkins)

It seems that Mrs Buckle and Mr Stephens also rolled a cheese each. There were seven races that year. It is interesting to note that Robert Perkins became MP for Stroud and at the start of the Second World War he joined the RAF as a Pilot Officer. By 1943 he had become a Flight Lieutenant.

1944

Six wooden cheeses would be rolled by:
Miss Ethel Priday
Mr Stephens
Dr Costley-White (Dean of Gloucester)
Revd D.E. Leavey
Mr C.W. Yates
Mr W. Jones

1945

Only four cheeses to be rolled by ladies:
Mrs Perkins
Mrs Buckle
Mrs Hall
Miss Priday

1946

Mr Robert Perkins (a civilian once more)
Mr Hicks-Beach (local landowner)
Dr Lowry (local GP)
Mr J.E. Morgan
Mr Stephens

1947

Maj. J. Davis
Mr C.R. Stephens
Dr H. Lowry
Mr W. Jones
Prizes were amended to: first 10s; second 5s; third 2s 6d.

1948

Maj. Hicks-Beach
Dr Lowry
Lt-Col. W. Davis
Miss Dorothy Pearson (an American teacher working at Denmark Road School, Gloucester)

Revd Stewart Bruce. (Rosemary Cooke)

1949

Mrs Hicks-Beach
Dr Lowry
Lt-Col. W.J. Davis
Revd de Lacey Mann
Col. Thompson

1950

Maj. Hicks-Beach
Dr Lowry
Mr C. Comley
Mr H. Carpenter
It can be noted that each year a doctor has appeared on the rollers list. This was to ensure that emergency medical treatment would be available if needed.

1951

Col. Thompson
Mr R. Mitchell
Mr J.P. Burroughs
Mr W. Jones

1952

Mr W.G. Knight

Mrs Millard
Dr Lowry or Dr Cookson
Mrs Kinton

1953

Whit Monday was a working day, due to the Coronation holiday. It was decided that only three cheeses would be rolled:
Mrs D.M. Johnstone
Dr Bradford
Major John Davis

1954

'After some discussion, it was decided that as cheese was now de-rationed, efforts should be made to obtain at least one real cheese to be the first one rolled.' (taken from the minutes of the committee 1954).

Lt. Col. W. Davis
Rear Admiral Bevan
Dr Linaker
Mr M.B. Watt (Supt St John's Ambulance)

1955

Mr P.R. Sullivan-Taylor
Mrs Reeder (South Africa)
Dr Millard
Revd Stewart Bruce (vicar of Brockworth)

1956

Mr Peter Scott
Dr J. Bronowski
Dr Lowry
Major John Davis
Dr Bronowski was a scientist who, through his television programme *The Ascent of Man* broadcast in the 1970s, did much to bring his subject to people in their homes. From 1956, there have been records available of rollers other than committee minutes.

1957

Mrs J. Lowry (Division Commissioner of Gloucestershire Girl Guides)
Mr Tony Pither (local farmer later to become committee chairman)
Miss E. Giblett (Cooper's Hill resident)
Wing-Commander Huntley Sinclair (Lord Baden-Powell, son of the founder of the Scout movement) was invited but was unable to attend.

Dr J. Bronowski rolling in 1956. (Roy Mitchell)

Maj. John Davis. (Roy Mitchell)

Miss Giblett about to roll the cheese with Ted Millard (MC 1956-1973). (*The Citizen*)

1958

Maj. Searight
Col. J.P. Calne
Lt-Col. W.J Davis (Cooper's Hill resident)
Dr D.C. Bradford

1959

Dr Linaker
Col. Guy
Mrs William Davis
Supt Dent (St John's Ambulance)

1960

Mr Look (cheese maker who donated one cheese)
Dr Millard
Mrs William Davis
Mr William Knight

1961

Five cheeses were offered so five races were to be run – four downhill and one uphill.
Dr H.J. Hoyland
Mr R. Look (of Shepton Mallet who presented four cheeses)
Mrs William Davis
Mr P. Rickards (Cooper's Hill resident)
Mrs W. Davis

1962

Miss Margaret Hill (employee of cheese maker)
Dr J. Brayshaw
Mrs C. Comely
Mr H. Mitchell

1963

Dr Bennett
Miss A. Knight
Major N. Warry

1964

Mr J. Morgan
Dr Bartlett
Mrs J. Coates
Mr Cushnan (chairman of the parish council)

1965

Mr A. Davis
Mrs E. Henson
Dr Bradford
Dr van Lottom

1966

Mr Tony Pither (later to become committee chairman)
Dr J. Hoyland
Mrs D. Embling (mayor)
Mr K.D. Brockhurst (chairman of the parish council)

1967

Mr Guy Davis (clerk to the county council)
Dr Garstang (Hucclecote)
Mrs Hewlett

Right: Dr H.J. Hoyland. *(The Citizen)*

Below: Mrs William Davis rolling for the ladies' race in 1961. (*The Citizen*)

Dr J. Brayshaw in 1962. (*The Citizen*)

Miss Knight rolls for the ladies, 1963. (*The Citizen*)

Major N.J. Warry rolling in 1963. (*The Citizen*)

Revd R.A. Norman

Prizes for the uphill race would be: first a cheese of up to £1 in value; second 7s 6d; third 5s.

1968

Inspector E. Bradbeer
Dr J.H. Lister
Mrs Ekeblad
Mr Roger Muirhead (Cooper's Hill resident)

1969

Ex-Sgt P.V. Falconer
Dr J.W. Bennett
Mrs Elizabeth Bruce
Mr J. Hanson (head of Brockworth Comprehensive School)

1970

Revd J.H. Haile
Dr F. Millard
Mrs D. Weston
Mr S. Croucher (Cooper's Hill resident)

1971

Maj. W. Clarke
Dr P.H. Tatham
Miss K. Johnstone (Cooper's Hill resident)
Mr K.R. Haslam (head of Brockworth Junior School)
Due to decimalisation prizes for downhill and uphill races were changed: second prize 50p; third prize 30p.

1972

Mr B. Mitchell
Dr D.C. Bradford
Mrs Simpson
Mr Tincello (warden of Brockworth Sports Centre)

1973

Mr John Workman (of Sheepscombe)
Dr J.W. Bennett
Mrs P. Phelps
Mr W.D. Vaughan (Brockworth Group scout master)

Mr Tony Pither with Ted Millard MC, 1966. (*The Citizen*)

1974

Dr P. Baddeley
Miss W. Taylor
Revd John Thornton (vicar of Bentham)
Mr J. James (head of Brockworth Comprehensive School) rolled a cheese presented by the family of the late Ted Millard who was MC from 1956-1973.

1975

Mr Wyatt (county land agent)
Dr Harbottle
Mrs C. Martell (cheese maker)
Mr P. Whittaker

1976

Mr Hicks Beach
Dr W. Goss
Mrs Rosemary J. Hellerman (Cooper's Hill resident)
Mr C.L. Cooper

1977

Rev Peter Naylor
Dr S. Steinhardt (Abbotswood Surgery)
Mrs P. Harding
Mr David Hardwick (Well Close Farm)

1978

Cllr Charles Lynch (chairman of the parish council)
Dr Charles Garstang
Mrs Hilda Poole
Mr Tim Johnson (warden)
The uphill race was cancelled because of the poor state of the hill.

1979

Mr Alan Morgan (churchwarden)
Dr D. Bradford
Mrs Croucher (Cooper's Hill resident)
Revd G. Whitehead (United Reform church)
The uphill race was again cancelled.

1980

Mr Wm. Organ
A doctor from Brockworth practice
Mrs Croucher
The warden of Horsbere House
There was no uphill race.

1981

Mr C. Fresney
Dr P. Swindell (vice principal of Star Centre, Ullenwood)
Mrs Margaret Millard (president of Cooper's Hill WI)
Mr H. Metson
For the fourth year in succession there was no uphill race.

1982

Mr Paul Marland MP.
Mr Islwyn John (record holder of the most wins – thirteen cheeses!)
This was the year when a thunderstorm interrupted the proceedings and cheeses were rolled in quick succession. As a result, Mrs Margaret McWalter (Cooper's Hill resident) and Dr N Patton, two invited rollers, did not roll their cheeses and were invited to return in 1983. Bill Organ rolled the second cheese and David Hardwick rolled the third. Cash prizes were increased: second £1; third 50p.

1983

Mr A. Morgan
Dr A. Watkins
Mrs Betty Bromage (Cooper's Hill resident)
Mr L. Griffiths
Once more there was no uphill race.

1984

Mrs E. McGrory (in memory of her father Col. Davis)
Dr Hoyland
Mr Harmer
Mr N. Crisp (cheese maker)
It seems that one of these rollers was replaced by Mr Geoff Newcombe. After a gap of six years an uphill race was introduced for children up to the age of twelve.

1985

Mr J. Gorod
Dr I. Smith
Mrs Searight
Mr J. Prior (mayor of Tewkesbury)

1986

Maj. Patrick Davis (Cooper's Hill resident)
Dr J. Lavric
Mrs E. Cooper
Mr J. Needham (warden of sports centre)
Prizes for the uphill races were revised: first prize a cheese to the value of £2; second prize £1; third prize 50p.

1987

Dr James Hoyland
Mr M. Reuby (warden of Gloucestershire Nature Conservation)
Mrs Jo du Feu (Cooper's Hill resident)
Mr Brian Millard (Cooper's Hill resident)

1988

Father John Brennan (St Patrick's RC church)
Dr F. Millard
Miss Joyce Flowers (Cooper's Hill resident)
Mr S. Pullen
Downhill prizes were revised: second £3; third £1. Uphill prizes were also revised – second £2; third £1.

1989

Mr James McGrory (Cooper's Hill resident)
Dr D. Maxted
Mrs D. Smart (cheese maker)
Mr W. Griffiths (Cardiff)

Above left: Mrs Elizabeth Davis. (Jean Jefferies)

Above right: Charles Coates. (Jean Jefferies)

1990

Mr Stephen Bick (in memory of Arthur Bick, MC since 1973)
Dr P. Arnold
Mrs J. Prior
Mr Mike Allen (head of Castle Hill School)

1991

Dr Massoud Khan
Mrs Joy Macdonald
Mr John Sewell
Mr H.J. Wyatt
Prizes were again revised. Downhill – second £5; third £3. Uphill – second £4; third £2.

1992

Dr M. Khan
Mr Richard Jefferies (Cooper's Hill resident)
Mrs E Davis (Cooper's Hill resident)
Mr R. Spencer

Richard Jefferies, a roller in 1992, is seen here with Rob Seex, MC from 1990 and David Hardwick (holding the programme), farmer and committee member. (Jean Jefferies)

1993

Revd W. Boon
Dr Mary Collick (Cooper's Hill resident)
Mrs Pam Holman
Mr Bob Bromberg (head of Castle Hill School)
The uphill race was so popular that it was decided to have three, one each for boys and girls as well as the open uphill.

1994

Mrs Pauline Carter
Mr Frank Trivett
Mrs Katherine Mulcahy (in memory of her father Brian Millard)
Mr Colin Burn (Cooper's Hill resident)

1995

Revd Martin Ennis
Mr M. Connolly (Cotswold Countryside Services)
Miss Muriel Fagg (Cooper's Hill resident)
Mr D. Bradford

1996

Mr Gordon Clifford
Mr Graham Ford (Cooper's Hill resident)
Mrs Pat Davis (parish council)
Mr Philip Bevan

1997

Mr Tony Pither (committee chairman)
Mr N. Negus
Mrs P. Morgan
Mr E. Hunt

1998

Mrs E. Davis rolled the only cheese at the early morning event that was held by local residents. The main event had to be cancelled for safety reasons.

1999

Mr G. Hall
Revd W. Perry
Mrs E. Ashenden (formerly Davis, Cooper's Hill resident)
Mr W. Parker
Prizes were revised. Downhill – second £5; third £3. Boys and girls uphill – second £2; third £1.50. Open uphill – second £4; third £2.

2000

Mr Charles Coates (county property manager)
Cllr Mark Hendry
Mrs Joan Stevens (local resident)
Maj. Richard Ashenden (Cooper's Hill resident)
In 2000, certificates were introduced for first, second and third places in each race.

2001

A nationwide outbreak of foot-and-mouth disease amongst cattle resulted in the cancellation of the year's event. Many other traditional events throughout the country suffered a similar fate. A single cheese was rolled by the committee later in the year to keep the tradition alive.

2002

This was the year of the Queen's Golden Jubilee. As celebrations were being held on Monday the Cheese Rolling and Wake was held on the Tuesday.
Revd David Primrose
Peter Bungard

Left: Mark Hendry. (Jean Jefferies)

Below: Major Richard Ashenden receives last-minute advice from MC Rob Seex. (Liz Ashenden)

Revd R. Mitchell in 2005.
(Malcolm Hopkins)

Mrs Alison Summerskill
Mrs Kate Harwood

2003

Unfortunately safety cover was unavailable as Rapid UK (the team required for helping casualties off the hill for first aid treatment) was on a mission in Algeria where there had been an earthquake. The official event was therefore cancelled. An unofficial event did take place (causing some chaos on the lanes) but no details are available.

2004

Guy Pither
Mike Wakeman
Mrs B. Wiltshire
J. Hunt

2005

Revd R. Mitchell
Andy Wakeham
Jean Jefferies
Derek Hayward

Jean Jefferies. (Malcolm Hopkins)

Derek Hayward. (Malcolm Hopkins)

Because of the increase in numbers of those wanting to take part in the competitions the number of men's races was increased from four to five. It was also decided to have four uphill races – boys under twelve years, girls under twelve years, a men's race and a women's race. Rollers for the downhill races were:

Sara Catlow-Hawkins (deputy head of Brockworth Enterprise School)
Adrian Jones (general manager of Prinknash Abbey)
Sue Burn (Cooper's Hill resident and teacher)
Neil Smith (a financial director and advisor to the Cheese Rolling Committee)
Amelia Hardwick (Cooper's Hill resident)

Sara Catlow-Hawkins. (Jean Jefferies)

Adrian Jones. (Jean Jefferies)

Neil Smith. (Jean Jefferies)

Amelia Hardwick. (Jean Jefferies)

ten

Winners

Names of early winners have been difficult to trace and some of the quotes cannot be verified. Many results have been taken from newspaper reports. While every effort has been made to verify names and spellings, I apologise for any errors or inaccuracies.

1870
Mr W.R. Organ claimed to have followed a cheese years before when he was 'a lad of 17'.

1907
Mr Alfred Cornwall, last heard of as living in Llantwit Major, won a cheese in about 1907.

1936
Jean Smith won the ladies' race.

1937
Bert Gregory claimed that as a lad, he had won six cheeses in one evening. Having chased cheeses for a quarter of a century he won more than any other person in the district with the possible exception of Jim Twinning of Cheltenham.

1937
Richard Luker
Tom Windo

1938

(28lb Double Gloucester cheese)
Leslie Hawkins (Tredworth) won two cheeses
Miss K. Dowson
Richard Luker
Mr H.C. Willington

1939

C.H. Willington
Miss K. Dowson
Leslie Hawkins (winner on two previous occasions)
Richard Luker (winner on two previous occasions)

1940

Keith Parsons won a 7lb cheese and later sold it for 1s per pound
William Haile (Tredworth) won his sixth cheese in five years
K. Parsons
Miss Ethel Hannis (Cranham) 'carried off the cheese in both the maiden's races'

The Whitsun bank holiday was cancelled because of the war, so there was a smaller crowd at the event.

1941

Patrick Townsend won two cheeses
Ilse Koeppler
Lance-Corporal Frew (a race that the army had to themselves)

This was the first year that the wooden substitute cheese was used in place of a real one and money prizes were given (see Chapter Five). The winner of each race had to return the cheese to the top of the hill for the next race. The wooden substitute was used for fourteen years until 1955 when real cheese was once again 'on the menu'!

1942

Patrick Townsend
Ilse Koeppler
Joan Chapman won one of the mixed races
Roy Mitchell won two cheeses

1943

Rosemary Smart (Astman /Hellerman)
John Astman
Roy Mitchell won two cheeses
William Hicks (Hucclecote)
Miss Ilse Koeppler won one of the events that was open to all
Alfred Butler (Gloucester)

1945

Results have not been found

1946

Michael Searight
John Salter
Reg Billingham
Jean Simpson
Tony Lowe won the uphill race

1947

Ronald Beamish won two cheeses
Raymond Payne
Jean Ward

1948

Roy Mitchell won two cheeses
M.J. Russell
Jean Simpson

Roy Mitchell lived in a cottage at the foot of the Cheese Roll slope, and became rather a legend.
He completed all his wins without falling and remained on his feet throughout all his contests.

1949

Roy Mitchell won his tenth cheese
J. Binder
Betty Hunt
Bernard Morgan

Left: Ronald Beamish who won two races in 1947.

Below left: Roy Mitchell won two cheeses in 1948. (Roy Mitchell)

Below right: Michael Price was a winner in 1954, 1955 and 1956. He won the first real cheese rolled since the Second World War.

1950

T. Brewster (Witcombe)
H. Ireland
Ken Davis (Bentham)
Miss M.E. Light (Sheepscombe)
Bernard Morgan

1951

Tom Holliday
M.C. Pinchin
Jean MacDonald
J. Bailey

1952

Tom Holliday (Great Witcombe)
Hilary Cooke (twelve years old from Chalford)
Hugh Atkinson (eleven years old from Hucclecote)
Tom Holliday also won the uphill race

1953

Rosemary Cooke (Longlevens) won 10s in the ladies' race
Tom Holliday
Ronald Ray (Coney Hill)

1954

Michael Price (Witcombe) won the first real cheese to be rolled since the Second World War. It was a 28lb Cheshire cheese which broke up as it reached the bottom of the hill. It was the only real cheese to be rolled. The wooden replica was rolled in the other races. Elke Ellaway was presented with a 5lb Dutch cheese by Admiral Sir Richard Bevan Eric Avent and Hugh Atkinson each received 10s for their winnings.

1955

Michael Price
Hugh Atkinson
Roy Holliday
Rosemary Cooke (Longlevens)

Real cheeses were rolled in all the races for the first time since the war and food rationing. They were 30lb New Zealand Cheddar cheeses and were provided by the New Zealand Dairy Products Marketing Commission.

Above left: Rosemary Cooke, winner in 1953, 1955 and 1956. (Jean Jefferies)

Above right: Rosemary Cooke.

Left: Paul Quarry in 1961. (*The Citizen*)

Roger Windo, a winner in 1962.
(*The Citizen*)

1956

Michael Price
Hugh Atkinson
Glyn Jenkins (Churchdown)
Rosemary Cooke won an 8lb Caerphilly cheese

It would seem that Rosemary Cooke, who now lives in Canada, may hold the ladies' record (at this point) of three wins and one second place. Her winning races were in 1953 with a prize of 10s, 1955 and 1956. When Rosemary visited England in 1999 she was asked 'Would you do it again?' Her answer was 'no!'

1957

Izzy John (Brockworth) won two cheeses
Hugh Atkinson
Frank Faulkner
June Wheeler

1958

Islwyn John won three cheeses (he declined to run in the third race)
Clive Walker (Brockworth)
Keith Anderson (Longlevens) won the uphill race
No ladies' race is mentioned

1959

Mary Bancroft

The Citizen of this date is missing so no other results are available.

1960

Islwyn John
Stanley Wilson-Copp (Witcombe)
Sheenan McBride (Innsworth)
Raymond Beard

1961

Islwyn John won two cheeses
Paul Quarry (Witcombe) won two cheeses

There was no ladies' race as there were no contestants.

1962

Paul Quarry won two cheeses (also won two in 1961 and two in 1962)
Roger Windo
Islwyn John

Once more there was no ladies' race.

1963

Roger Windo won two cheeses; second in the third race
Clive Whittaker
Mrs Pat Harding (daughter of Maj. and Mrs Searight, local residents)

Roger Windo was the grandson of Tom Windo who was MC from 1934-1955.

Above left: Islwyn (Izzy) John. (*The Citizen*)

Above middle: Raymond and Michael Giles, 1966. (*The Citizen*)

Above right: Richard Giles. (*The Citizen*)

Right: Diane Bowers was a winner in 1967 and 1969. (*The Citizen*)

Above left: Steve Lott in 1971. (*The Citizen*)

Above right: Deborah Harwood was the ladies' winner in 1972 and 1973. She ran again in 2000 but was not placed. (*The Citizen*)

1964

Clive Whittaker
Roger Windo
Izzy John
Julie Tiffany

Izzy John is reported to have won twelve cheeses over eight years. Records for 1961 are missing, but if he won two races that year (which is more than likely) this total would be correct. He won two cheeses in 1957 and 1968 and possibly won two in 1959. He also won in 1960, 1961 (two cheeses), 1962 and 1964.

1965

Raymond Giles (Brockworth)
Michael Davis (Hucclecote)
Janet Ballinger (Gloucester)
Clive Whittaker (Stroud)

Above left: Chris Woodhouse, winner in 1973. (*The Citizen*)

Above right: Patrick Hendzell (left) with his brother John who won in 1972. (*The Citizen*)

1966

Raymond Giles won two cheeses
Michael Giles
Janet Beesley

An extra 10s was presented to each winner by an anonymous donor.

1967

R.A. Copley (Brockworth)
Eric Huckins (Gloucester)
Diane Bowers
George Duckett

1968

Hugh Oxenham
Eric Huckins
Barbara Bayne (on holiday from Glamorgan)
Michael Giles

1969

Richard Giles won two cheeses
Joe Johnson (Shurdington)
Diane Bowers

1970

Richard Giles won two cheeses
Peter Davis (Cranham)
Lynda Burnett

1971

Steve Lott
Lynda Burnett (broke her collar-bone for the second year)
Peter Davis
Gordon Graham

1972

Steve Lott won two cheeses
Christopher Woodhouse
John Hendzell
Deborah Harwood

Right: Tony Hendzell. (*The Citizen*)

Opposite left: Susan Keavey. (*The Citizen*)

Opposite right: Paul Chandler broke his collar bone winning in 1975. (*The Citizen*)

1973

Chris Woodhouse (Tuffley)
Alan Thorpe (Brockworth)
Deborah Harwood (Brockworth)
Patrick Hendzell (Brockworth)
Justine Davis (Brockworth) won the uphill race

1974

Stephen Giles
Patrick Hendzell
Susan Keavey
Chris Woodhouse
Gary John won the uphill race

1975

Paul Chandler
Patrick Hendzell
Joanna Evans
Paul Brammer

1976

George Duckett (Witcombe)
Stephen Gyde
Joanna Evans
Paul Williams

1977

Tony Hendzell
David Lawlor
Megan Morris
Rory Martin

1978

Tony Hendzell (lost a front tooth)
John Lowe (Brockworth)
Janice McGrory (Brockworth)
Stephen Gyde (Brockworth)

1979

Stephen Gyde won two cheeses
Tony Hendzell
Candice Phillips – the only lady to run

1980

Stephen Gyde won all three cheeses
Mandy Day

1981

Kevin Gyde won two cheeses
Andy Fuller
Amanda Turner (Brockworth)

1982

Stephen Gyde won two cheeses
Amanda Turner
Kevin Gyde (Brockworth)

Johnathon Lowe won in 1978. (*The Citizen*)

Janice McGrory won the ladies' race in 1978. (*The Citizen*)

Kevin Gyde with a soggy cheese, winner in 1982. *(The Citizen)*

1983

Colin Hill (Brockworth)
Stephen Gyde
'Digger' Gardener (Gloucester)
Amanda Turner

Amanda holds the ladies' joint record (at this point) of three wins with Rosemary Cooke (1953, 1955, 1956).

1984

Stephen Gyde
Steven Brain
Claudia Dart
Ian Campbell

Amanda Turner. (*The Citizen*)

Above, left and right: Stephen Gyde, triple winner in 1980 and double winner in 1982. (*The Citizen*)

1985

Stephen Gyde won two cheeses
Costas Logothetis
Leticia Burns

1986

Steven Brain won two cheeses
Stephen Gyde
Leticia Burns

1987

Stephen Gyde
Steven Brain won two cheeses
Rebecca Haines (Crickley Hill)

1988

Stephen Gyde won two cheeses
Steven Brain
Rebecca Haines

1989

Paul Andres (Cashes Green)
Lawrence Farlow (Brockworth)
Kathleen Underwood
Julian Pritchard

1990

Stephen Gyde
Steven Brain
Jackie McGinn
Adam Pedley won the children's uphill race

1991

Stephen Gyde won all three cheeses and announced his retirement
Christie Sweeney (Tewkesbury) won the ladies' race
Stephen Gyde won twenty-one cheeses in fourteen years. Steven Brain won seventeen cheeses in ten years.

Right: Steven Brain. (Jean Jefferies)

Below left: Peter Astman, men's champion in 1998. (Jean Jefferies)

Below right: Amelia Hardwick. (Jean Jefferies)

Above left: Stephen Brain. (Jean Jefferies)

Above right: Craig Brown. (Jean Jefferies)

Left: Kirby Shepherd. (Jean Jefferies)

Above left: Dione Carter. (Jean Jefferies)

Above right: Stephen Gyde. (Jean Jefferies)

Right: Stephen Brain. (Jean Jefferies)

Above left: Jason Crowther. (Jean Jefferies)

Above right: Dionne Carter. (Jeremy Kaye)

Left: Hannah Jones. (Jeremy Kaye)

Craig Fairley. (Jean Jefferies)

Dione Carter. (Jean
Jefferies)

Chris Anderson. (Jean Jefferies)

Andrew Brewin. (Jean Jefferies)

1992

Terry Sawczuk (Brockworth)
Stuart Heggs (Abbeydale)
Rob Preece (Quedegley)
Star Royles (Brockworth)

1993

Rob Preece won two cheeses
Jamie Barnes (Brockworth)
Andrew Deveson (Brockworth)
Stephen Gyde came second in two races

1994

Rob Preece
Andrew Deveson
Star Royles
Craig Carter

1995

Steven Brain
Jonathan Smith (Bishops Cleeve)
Claire Carter (Brockworth)
Darren Yates (Brockworth)

1996

Steven Brain
Harry Hancy (Brockworth)
Marie Andow (Brockworth)
John Shelton (Hucclecote)

1997

Steve Brain won two cheeses (one of which was stolen)
Tina Rimmer (Brockworth)

Craig Carter broke his arm and had his cheese stolen while he was receiving first aid.

1998

This was a different year. Safety pressures meant that the public event had to be cancelled (see Chapter Two). To keep a continuity in the tradition, local residents held an unofficial event during the day. The winners of the single race were:

Peter Astman men's champion
Amelia Hardwick ladies' champion

1999

Steven Brain won three cheeses
Helen Thorpe
Victoria Burn won the girls' uphill race

2000

Steve Brain won two cheeses (bringing his total to seventeen)
Craig Brown
Kirby Shepherd

2001

There was no Cheese Rolling because an outbreak of foot-and-mouth disease had resulted in the closure of the countryside. However, when restrictions had been lifted at the end of July the committee rolled one cheese to uphold the tradition!

2002

Simon Fowler
Craig Brown
Saskia Thomas
Jack Williams

2003

An earthquake in Algeria meant that with no rescue team was available St John's Ambulance personnel had to withdraw from providing emergency cover for the day. As a result the committee had no choice but to cancel the event at short notice. Some people from the surrounding area organised their own races but no details are available.

2004

Padam Shreer (a soldier in the Royal Ghurka Regiment)
Marc Ellis (a player in the New Zealand All Blacks rugby team)
Dione Carter (from New Zealand)
Aaron Walden

Stephen Brain and Steven Gyde, old adversaries, both entered the first race.
Stephen Gyde, who holds the record for having won the most cheeses (twenty-one cheeses in fourteen years 1978-1991) was delighted to come third. Steven Brain, (with a total of seventeen cheeses in ten years between 1984-2000) unfortunately fell and broke his ankle.

2005

Jason Crowther
Chris Anderson
Dione Carter
Aaron Walden

Uphill winners:
Chris Calver-Jones
Hannah Jones
Adam Dunsford

2006

Jason Crowther
Craig Fairley
Dionne Carter (her third win)
Chris Anderson
Andrew Brewin
Uphill Races
Boys under twelves – Josh Prike
Girls under twelves – Kelley Beckett
Ladies uphill – Ruth Bradbrook
Men's uphill – Julian Gray

Conclusion

There is no conclusion!
As long as people come, the cheese will continue to roll!

Other local titles published by Tempus

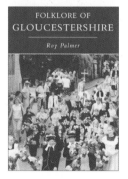

Folklore of the Cotswolds

JUNE LEWIS-JONES

This detailed book explores the heritage of folklore that has always been so prevalent throughout the Cotswolds, from cures and remedies, recipes and traditions to dance, song, music and mumming. It includes mysteries, tales of witches and ghosts, legends born of the landscape, such as the Devil's Chimney and the Rollright Stones, and lesser-known Cotswold stories like the secret marriage at Snowshill Manor.

0 7524 2930 2

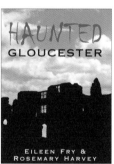

Folklore of Gloucestershire

ROY PALMER

Here are recounted tales inspired by landscape, village lore, legends, superstitions, stories of devils, fairies, witches and ghosts, sports and fairs, song and dance, revels and rituals. Roy Palmer is an acknowledged authority on the subject of folklore, and his work in collecting material from within the traditional boundaries of Gloucestershire is a major contribution to the historic records of the county.

0 7524 2246 4

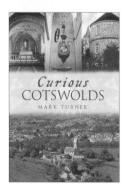

Haunted Gloucester

EILEEN FRY AND ROSEMARY HARVEY

From paranormal manifestations at Gloucester Docks to the ghostly activity of a monk who is said to haunt the city's twelfth-century Cathedral, this spine-tingling collection of supernatural tales recalls strange and spooky happenings in the city's ancient streets, churches, theatres and public houses, including The Kingsholm Inn and Bridge Inn. Here's a glimpse into the ghostly legacy of Gloucester's past.

0 7524 3312 1

Curious Cotswolds

MARK TURNER

In common with many parts of Britain, the Cotswolds has an abundance of curiosities. For those who are perennially attracted to anything that might be termed 'curious' – an ancient standing stone, a little-known beauty spot, a folly erected by some eccentric egotist, or, perhaps, the site of an unsolved murder – this book will satisfy even the most ardent enthusiast by uncovering some of the area's most fascinating people, places and events.

0 7524 3930 8

If you are interested in purchasing other books published by Tempus, or in case you have difficulty finding any Tempus books in your local bookshop, you can also place orders directly through our website

www.tempus-publishing.com